Mastering 3D STUDIO®
Modeling, Rendering, and Animation

Mastering 3D STUDIO®
Modeling, Rendering, and Animation

Jon M. Duff
Purdue University

William A. Ross
Purdue University

PWS Publishing Company

I(T)P An International Thomson Publishing Company

Boston • Albany • Bonn • Cincinnati • Detroit • London • Madrid • Melbourne
Mexico City • New York • Paris • San Francisco • Singapore • Tokyo • Toronto • Washington

PWS PUBLISHING COMPANY
20 Park Plaza, Boston, Massachusetts 02116-4324

Copyright © 1996 by PWS Publishing Company, a division of International Thomson Publishing Inc.

All rights reserved. No part of this book may be reproduced, stored in a retrieval system, or transmitted, in any form or by any means -- electronic, mechanical, photocopying, recording, or otherwise -- without the prior written permission of PWS Publishing Company.

3D Studio is a registered trademark of Autodesk, Inc.

 This book is printed on recycled, acid-free paper.

I(T)P ™
International Thomson Publishing
The trademark ITP is used under license.

For more information, contact:

PWS Publishing Co.
20 Park Plaza
Boston, MA 02116

International Thomson Publishing Europe
Berkshire House I68-I73
High Holborn
London WC1V 7AA
England

Thomas Nelson Australia
102 Dodds Street
South Melbourne, 3205
Victoria, Australia

Nelson Canada
1120 Birchmount Road
Scarborough, Ontario
Canada M1K 5G4

International Thomson Editores
Campos Eliseos 385, Piso 7
Col. Polanco
11560 México D.F., Mexico

International Thomson Publishing GmbH
Königswinterer Strasse 418
53227 Bonn, Germany

International Thomson Publishing Asia
221 Henderson Road
#05-10 Henderson Building
Singapore 0315

International Thomson Publishing Japan
Hirakawacho Kyowa Building, 31
2-2-1 Hirakawacho
Chiyoda-ku, Tokyo 102
Japan

Library of Congress Cataloging-in-Publication Data

Duff, Jon M.
  Mastering 3D Studio : modeling, rendering, and animation / Jon M. Duff, William A. Ross.
    p.   cm.
  Includes index.
  ISBN 0534-95136-8
  1. Computer animation. 2. 3D studio. 3. Computer graphics.
I. Ross, William A. II. Title.
TR897.7.D84   1995   95-45802
006.6--dc20   CIP

Sponsoring Editor: Jonathan Plant
Production Coordinator: Robine Andrau
Marketing Development Manager: Nathan Wilbur
Manufacturing Coordinator: Wendy Kilborn
Assistant Editor: Ken Morton
Interior Designer: The WestHighland Press

Cover Designer: Julia Gecha
Cover Art: Image created by Robert Stein III,
  AniGraF/X, courtesy Autodesk®, Inc.
  Copyright 1994
Cover Printer: John P. Pow Co.
Text Printer: Courier/Westford

Printed and bound in the United States of America
95 96 97 98 99 -- 10 9 8 7 6 5 4 3 2 1

Table of Contents

Preface ix

Chapter 1 Introduction

1.1	The Animation Process	2
1.2	Concept Development	5
1.3	Model Construction	7
1.4	Scene Layout	9
1.5	Animation Setup	11
1.6	Final Editing	11
1.7	Using the Lab Sheets	12
1.8	Questions to Answer	20

Chapter 2 Modeling

2.1	Understanding Modeling	22
2.2	You Must Know Space	26
2.3	Approaches to Modeling	27
2.4	Use Predefined Primitives	28
2.5	Create a Profile	28
2.6	Create a Lofted Extrusion	29
2.7	Create a Swept Shape	30
2.8	Boolean Union	30
2.9	Boolean Subtraction	31
2.10	Boolean Intersection	32
2.11	CAD Models	33
2.12	Modeling Exercises	34
2.13	Questions to Answer	36

Chapter 3 Rendering

3.1	Understanding Rendering	44
3.2	Influence of Light Sources	49
3.3	Importance of Materials	52
3.4	Material Maps	55
3.5	Detail! Detail! Detail!	55
3.6	Environment	56
3.7	Rendering Cues	57
3.8	Photorealistic Rendering	58
3.9	Rendering Exercises	62
3.10	Questions to Answer	62

Chapter 4 Animation

4.1	Introduction	70
4.2	An Animation as a Stage Play	70
4.3	Storyboarding	72
4.4	Key Frame Animation	74
4.5	You Must Know the Camera	76
4.6	Everything Moves	78
4.7	Morphing	81
4.8	Animation Formats	83
4.9	Animation Exercises	84
4.10	Questions to Answer	84

Chapter 5 Product Detail

5.1	Introduction	92
5.2	Your Assignment	92
5.3	Your Project Notebook	95
5.4	Storyboards	96
5.5	Model Construction	96
5.6	Scene Layout	98
5.7	Animation Setup and Key Frames	98
5.8	Finished Animation Materials	98
5.9	Alternative Assignments	99

Chapter 6 Product Assembly

6.1	Introduction	102
6.2	Project Description	102
6.3	Storyboards	104
6.4	Project Notebook	104
6.5	Model Construction	104
6.6	Scene Layout	105
6.7	Animation Setup and Key Frames	106
6.8	File Organization	107
6.9	Finished Materials	107
6.10	Alternate Assignments	108

Chapter 7 Process Model

7.1	Introduction	110
7.2	Project Description	112
7.3	Model Planning Sketch	116
7.4	Project Notebook	116
7.5	Storyboards	116
7.6	Scene Layout	117

7.7	File Organization	118
7.8	Finished Materials	118
7.9	Alternative Assignments	119

Chapter 8 Walk-Through

8.1	Introduction	128
8.2	Project Description	130
8.3	Project Design	130
8.4	Model Planning Sketch	135
8.5	Project Notebook	136
8.6	Scene Layout	137
8.7	Alternative Assignments	138

Chapter 9 Product Logo

9.1	Introduction	140
9.2	Project Description	140
9.3	Project Design and Development	142
9.4	Finished Materials	143
9.5	Scene Layout	144
9.6	Alternative Assignments	145
	Index	146
	Planning Sheets	149

Preface

Welcome to *Mastering 3D Studio*! This book and the software open to you the amazing world of computer rendering and animation. It is a world populated only by the limits of your imagination. Things that are impossible in our world are entirely possible in the virtual world of 3D Studio.

Successful animation requires creativity, computer knowledge, and careful planning. It also requires an understanding of modeling, materials, rendering, lighting, motion, and cameras. You can achieve amazing results very quickly—almost without knowing what you are doing. But there is a big difference between something flashy with little significance and something of lasting value you can really be proud of.

The chapters in this book are organized to encourage an understanding of computer animation that will ultimately result in successful, effective animations. The first four chapters are meant to be read **while you are completing the tutorial assignments included with your 3D Studio software**. This should take from 2 to 4 weeks in a normal classroom setting. Along with the readings are drawing and sketching activities that you will rely on later when you begin the actual animation assignments.

The chapters make references to the 3D Studio *Reference Manual* and the 3D Studio *Installation Guide & Tutorial*. These three books work together; after you complete the tutorials, you will want to keep the *Reference Manual* close at hand because 3D Studio is such a robust product that there is no way you will be able to remember everything.

The assignments require you to produce both animations and static renderings and to compile a record of your work in a Project Notebook. To help you do this, we have provided blank sheets for planning, sketching, and recording your actions. You may at first think these are busy work, but rest assured, they are required in actual animation industries. If your ambition is to become a professional animator, potential employers will expect to see evidence of your planning. If you simply want to explore rendering and animation, this structured approach is invaluable in understanding the process.

If you are just beginning in the areas of modeling, rendering, and animation, there will be many new terms to learn. At the beginning of each chapter you will find a list of terms to know and define. Your best reference for these is your 3D Studio *Reference Manual*. Although it doesn't have a glossary as such, students may find that a quick trip to the index will reveal that the first page entry where a term is introduced is usually where it is defined. Of greater importance is your ability to define these terms in your own words, with your own understanding, *after*

you have engaged in the activities of the chapter. By compiling your own glossary chapter by chapter, you will develop a strong vocabulary in animation.

At the end of each chapter you will find a list of questions to answer. These require research in the 3D Studio references and other sources as necessary. Many of these questions don't have single correct answers. They are intended to encourage you to start thinking and speaking as a digital animator.

As a reminder, this book is keyed directly to the 3D Studio *Tutorial Guide* and 3D Studio *Reference Manual*. Each chapter of this book includes a specific reading assignment in the *Reference Manual* and specific exercises in the *Tutorial Guide*. Additionally, where critical passages in each of these references would clarify points or assignments the appropriate passages are identified with *Tutorial* and *Reference* buttons.

Have fun!

Jon M. Duff
William A. Ross

Acknowledgments

The authors are grateful for the many hours of professional review given this book by the following reviewers:

Edward Anderson
Texas Tech University

Lamar Henderson
Catholic University

Bisi Oladipupo
Hampton University

James Shahan
Iowa State University

We hope that the approach to rendering and animation we have developed will serve your students well. The continuing advice and support from Roger Payne of Autodesk and Jonathan Plant of PWS Publishing were important factors in bringing this to a successful completion. And, finally, thanks to our students at Purdue, many of whom are now employed in engineering, architectural, industrial, and design firms, doing what they love to do.

Preface

Credits

Color Plates

Gallery 1	Jeff Hannah
Gallery 2	Dave Gevers
Gallery 3	Dave Gevers
Gallery 4	Aaron Cover, Heather Alvey
Gallery 5	Aaron Cover, Heather Alvey
Gallery 6	Shawn Coffing
Gallery 7	Shawn Coffing
Gallery 8	Paul Wing
Gallery 9	Paul Wing
Gallery 10	Tim Brummett
Gallery 11	Jeff Hanna
Gallery 12	Jeff Hanna
Gallery 13	Chris Freeman, Matt Harshbarger, Aaron Voelker
Gallery 14	Chris Freeman, Matt Harshbarger, Aaron Voelker

Chapter 1

Opener	Shawn Coffing
1-1	Charles T. Parsons
1-3	Wen-Lan Chou
1-4	David Snyder
1-5	Ron Stephany
1-6	Keith Ballard

Chapter 2

Opener	Chris Burden, Scott Martin, Christina Moehle, Brad Slott
2-2	Aaron Cover
2-3	Chris Burden, Scott Martin, Christina Moehle, Brad Slott

Chapter 3

3-1	Aaron Cover
3-2	Tim Brummett
3-3	Shawn Coffing
3-6	Rudy Arrendondo
3-10	Jeff Hanna
3-11	Chris Burden, Scott Martin, Christina Moehle, Brad Slott

Chapter 4

Opener	Aaron Cover
4-1	Aaron Cover
4-2	Shawn Coffing
4-3	Shawn Coffing
4-8	Jeff Ello

Preface

4-11	Chris Burden, Scott Martin, Christina Moehle, Brad Slott

Chapter 5
5-2	Erin Cornell
5-4	Erin Cornell

Chapter 6
Opener	Paul Wing, Dan Goodman, Tim Asher
6-1	*Snowmobile:* Dave Friedrich, Dave Vislosky, Mike Long, Chad Snoeberger
	Vise: Shawn Coffing, David Ham, Keith Kirschling
	Flashlight: Nate Hartman, Damon Lowell, Cory Powell, Marty Rupp
6-2	*Shock Absorber:* Milke Long
	Flashlight: Nate Hartman, Damon Lowell, Cory Powell, Marty Rupp
	Vise: Shawn Coffing, David Ham, Keith Kirschling
6-3	*Coffee Maker:* Jennifer DeFries, Don Herzog, Nicole Meyer, Stephen Rees

Chapter 7
Opener	Jeff Hanna
7-1	Shawn Coffing
7-7	Brett Burkhart

Chapter 8
Opener	Jeff Hanna
8-1	Jeff Hanna
8-4	Jeff Hanna

Chapter 9
Opener	Jeff Ello
9-1	*Soup Shootout:* Eric Davis
	Logo: Wen-Lan Chow

All other figures by the authors.

Chapter 1

Introduction

1 Introduction

1.1 The Animation Process

As an animation student, you probably need experience in more related and unrelated areas than any fellow student you know. You have to know hardware, software, color models, **raster** and **vector** methods, **digital** and **analog** video and audio, lights, cameras, and theater-like scene creation and action (Figure 1-1). The simple truth is that you can't develop the same level of ability in all of these areas—potential employers, if they are fair to you, won't expect that either.

However, there are several topics in which you need to be well versed in order to function as an animator. The first part of this book is devoted to raising your awareness of what skills teachers and potential employers generally agree are fundamental to the process.

There! We said it! Animation is firstly a *process*. A product (the animation) is the surely the result of that process. You may get your first animation job at least partially on the basis of a finished animation. You will *keep* that job and move on to positions of increasing responsibility and creative potential based on your understanding of the animation process. If you know process, materials, and equipment, and if you have your share of creative ability, you *will* produce effective animation (Figure 1-2).

An animation happens when images change over time. This change may be the result of altering the viewer's position (camera), moving the object through space over time (**translation**), changing lighting, or actually deforming the object over time (**morphing**). The objects don't have to be three-dimensional; they don't even have to be realistic. But for the purposes of the exercises in this book, **animation** is considered to be a series of **rendered** still frames assembled in such an order that, when viewed in rapid succession, natural continuous motion is perceived (Figure 1-3). Therefore, the precursor of animation is rendering. Chapter 3 discusses rendering in detail and introduces short exercises that reinforce these rendering concepts.

This book concentrates on *technical animation*. A technical animation is used to show form or function and to aid in design, manufacturing, construction, assembly, training, or marketing. 3D Studio can also be used for creative animation, and many of you will experiment with dancing French fries and marching celery stalks.

Terms to Know and Define

analog
copyright
digital
focal length
hierarchical links
HLS color
maps
materials
model geometry
morphing
raster
render
RGB color
storyboard
translation
vector

The Animation Process

The production and evaluation of an animation is a time-consuming and oftentimes expensive proposition. It is important that you understand the process and be able to visualize its steps. It's important to fully understand the process of animation. If you feel comfortable with the process, changes in tools or equipment will seem less traumatic.

- Concept Development and Storyboards

- Model Construction

- Scene Layout

- Animation Setup

- Final Editing and Compositing

Figure 1-1 **Lighting the Scene.** *Scene rendered with effective lighting. Note the use of back and directional lighting that results in theater-like realism.*

Planning Stage
File Organization Sheet (page 16)
In this stage, you analyze the desired results of the process. Is your goal to produce photorealistic stills or full-motion animations? What is the intended delivery medium? How will the product be used? What is the audience? Make a quick trip to the Output Stage to determine the form of the final product.

Modeling Stage
Model Planning Sheet (page 14)
In this stage you determine what geometries will be necessary to accomplish the task. Decisions made in the Planning Stage impact the level of detail needed in the models. It is appropriate here to plan the use of maps to achieve the visual detail you need. You will create profiles in 3D Studio's Shaper, extrude and sweep the profiles in the Lofter, and combine these geometries with primitives and imported dxf models in the 3D Editor.

Prerendering Stage
Objects and Materials Sheet (page 18)
Cameras and Lighting Sheet (page 17)
The location of cameras and lights directly impact the detail and application of materials and maps. You want to plan the most efficient use of objects and materials by sharing both geometry and maps whenever possible. In this stage you have the opportunity to return to the previous two stages as necessary to make adjustments. You will use 3D Studio's Materials Editor to create materials and maps and set cameras and lights in the 3D Editor.

Animation Stage
Animation Storyboard (page 15)
Frame Planning Sheet (page 19)
This stage encourages planning the animation so that desired results can be achieved. The key frames are sketched on storyboards and the movement of lights, cameras, and objects is orchestrated frame by frame. This information is then used in the Keyframer module in 3D Studio to create the animation.

Output Stage
It is helpful to know the intended output early in the process. Many modeling, rendering, and animation decisions hinge on this knowledge. You will need to choose appropriate file formats, resolutions, and palettes.

Figure 1-2 **Animation Process.** *An animation combines geometry, materials, and lighting with the temporal element that allows objects, cameras, and lights to move and change over time. The process encourages preplanning but allows for feedback as necessary.*

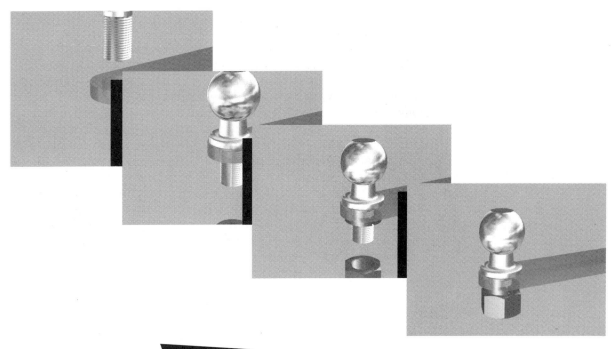

Figure 1-3 **Animation Frames.** *A sequence of rendered frames that when assembled can result in an animation.*

1.2 Concept Development

In order to coordinate an animation, the job needs to be specified in unambiguous terms. Many questions arise during the course of an animation project. Without exact project specifications, the client may be unhappy with the final results. Most companies don't last long with unhappy clients. Can you answer the following questions.

- What is the purpose of the animation?
- What is the medium of final delivery?
- How will the animation be displayed?
- Who gets possession of the final electronic files?
- What rights, if any, are reserved by the animator?
- Is there a review process? If so, what is it?

1 Introduction

Many problems that surface during the actual animation procedure can be worked out with the use of sketches and **storyboards**. A storyboard (Figure 1-4) is a way of communicating first impressions about geometry, camera position, lighting, and **materials** *before* time is invested in actually animating. These sketched storyboards are not only quick to produce, but an animator also has less investment in the product (after all, it's a sketch!). The storyboard promotes dialogue between members of the team and the client. If you are interviewing for a job in animation and can show a potential employer professional quality storyboards *and* the finished animation, your chances for getting hired have just gone up dramatically! Note that I referred to them as *professional* quality storyboards. Throughout this book you will find examples of storyboards produced by successful animators. Copy them, emulate them, memorize them.

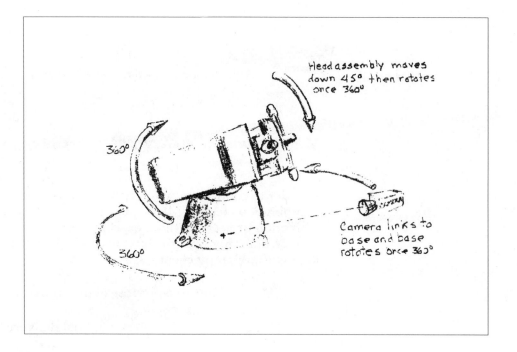

Figure 1-4 **An Effective Storyboard.** Notice that an effort has been made to describe geometric form, movement, and lighting.

You should keep a *notebook* for each animation project. This notebook will contain the following:

- The animation specification
- All communications between you and the client
- Model and file planning sheets
- Storyboard sketches
- Rendered key frames
- Animation files or a complete description of their location

1.3 Model Construction

3-1 through 3-8
4-1 through 4-16

5-2, 6-2, 7-2

Chapter 2 covers modeling in detail and suggests short exercises that demonstrate modeling techniques. It is difficult to be an effective animator without being an effective modeler. This is because three-dimensional animations are based on valid three-dimensional surfaces. If you can't create valid, believable surfaces, the rendering engine in 3D Studio will have a difficult time making them look realistic. You'll have holes and gaps in your surfaces. Some surfaces will have outsides but no insides. Some surfaces will be inside out. Some surfaces won't be where you want them.

In 3D Studio and other similar electronic products, there is an interesting relationship between *modeled* geometry and *rendered* geometry. An effective animator will model only the minimum detail necessary to capture the physical nature of a subject. Other details (such as tire treads, screw threads, knurls, ribs, grooves, windows, dentals, etc.) are created at rendering time by the use of **maps**, a way of tricking the rendering engine into modifying color or value so that the appearance of surface deviation is achieved. Figure 1-5 shows **model geometry** and the finished image after mapping has added detail at rendering time.

An animation is by its nature an abstraction of a real-world or hypothetical situation. Therefore, proportional accuracy is of greater importance than precise mathematical accuracy. Some of the details take care of themselves if you use engineering data as the bases of your models. In fact, an engineering model may be

1 Introduction

too exact, too precisely defined for easy use in an animation program. You may need to abstract the engineering model yourself to get it in a form easily used in animation.

A word of caution about **copyright** and intellectual property. A model you find on the Internet, on an electronic bulletin board, or as part of an existing animation file is not a candidate for indiscriminate use. You have to consider that every piece of geometry you didn't make belongs to someone else. *Don't use someone else's work.* The same can be said about backgrounds, maps, and textures. If you *do* use stock raster images, make sure they are copyright-free or in the public domain. Either way, never try passing these off as your own. Acknowledge every source. Libraries are great for increasing your productivity but use them wisely.

Anyway, how would you like to be interviewing for a job, showing an animation to a potential employer that you think is really great, only to have the interviewer recognize a piece of your work as appearing earlier in _____ (you fill in the blank). You have to demonstrate that you can analyze, plan, sketch, model, render, and animate.

Readings

Tutorial   Tutorials 1 & 2

Reference Chapter 1-4
               Define terms at beginning of this chapter
               from Reference Index

Scene Layout

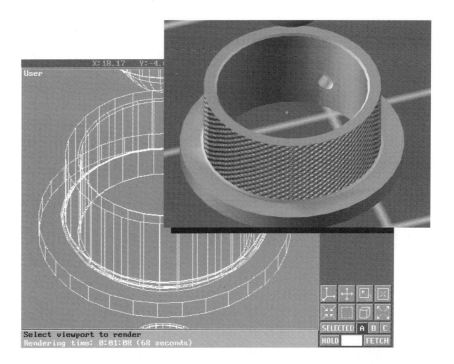

Figure 1-5 **Detail Using Maps.** *A model in the 3D Editor Module comprised of simple primitives with surface perturbations achieved at rendering time using bump maps.*

1.4 Scene Layout

TUTORIAL
13-3, 20-8

REFERENCE
7-3, 7-5, 7-12

As you will discover by working on the exercises in this book, an animation is really a process of assembling and placing objects into some kind of spatial orientation. Because these objects often don't come together in the same file until late in the modeling process, effective storyboards are all the more important. The selection of surface materials depends somewhat on the selection of background environment. Do you want the background reflected in one or more of the objects in the scene? Or would such reflections only confuse the viewer?

Understanding raster (bitmap) **materials** and **maps** is imperative to being a successful animator. Even if you have access to extensive libraries of materials and maps, you will need to create your own at some time. Your value to a company isn't based solely on intelligent selection of available maps. You have to demonstrate that you can create your own.

1 Introduction

Without effective lighting, an animation will appear dim, or flat, or, even worse, disappear altogether. This is an area of animation many companies delegate to individuals who really know how to set lights. But if you work in a company that can't afford such a luxury and you are the lighting expert by default, you will find that lighting adheres to the KISS principle: Keep It Simple Stupid. The greater number and more diverse the lights you add to a scene, the less detail is observable where sunlight, shade, and shadow can be seen within the same field of view. You want all three at the same time, all the time. If all of your scene is equally illuminated, it will look like a polar bear in a snowstorm. Figure 1-6 shows an effectively illuminated scene. Note how the placement of the lights brings out the three-dimensionality of the scene.

If you know something about still and video cameras, you will see that 3D Studio mimics their capabilities and overcomes some of their physical limitations. You should look for interesting and dramatic camera locations, angles, and **focal lengths**. Stop short of perspectives that, although they may satisfy your Hitchcockian director needs, leave viewers scratching their heads wondering, "What did I just see?"

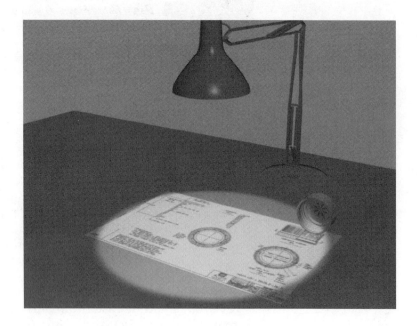

Figure 1-6 **Light Source Placement.** *An effectively illuminated scene. Note the placement of the light sources in the 3D Editor.*

You should be able to choose appropriate rendering and animation parameters for testing the validity of your modeling, mapping, and scene decisions. It tempting to overrender too many frames too early in the process. Why? Because you can. You must be able to demonstrate to your employer that you make effective and efficient use of both your time and that of your animation workstation.

1.5 Animation Setup

Until now, the animation exists as objects in space. You view the scene from a single vantage point in order to check the validity of how you interpreted your storyboards. A single vantage point can become a key frame that controls the position of geometry, lights, and cameras. 3D Studio interpolates between key frames based on your instructions as to how the objects (camera, lights, geometry) are altered.

15-1

8-4 through 8-6

Running the animation in preview mode allows you to edit the paths of cameras, lights, and objects until the desired results are achieved.

If you want certain objects to move in relation to other objects, you will establish **hierarchical links**. These parent-child relationships are instrumental in animating mechanical or architectural assemblies. Figure 1-7 shows an object in which moving one part (the parent) causes the movement of another (the child).

Based on the information in your animation specifications, you will select output characteristics and formats and render the frames. You should have already rendered a sampling of the frames to your monitor and run a sufficient number of previews so that the actual rendered animation will contain few, if any, surprises.

1.6 Final Editing

These final steps in the animation process are often called "post-processing" because they are what you do to your animation pieces to achieve a final product. You will want to break up large animations into short segments. It is difficult to load, display, save, render to the screen, and run animation sequences that are longer than three or four seconds at 30 frames per second on any but the most robust animation workstations.

1 Introduction

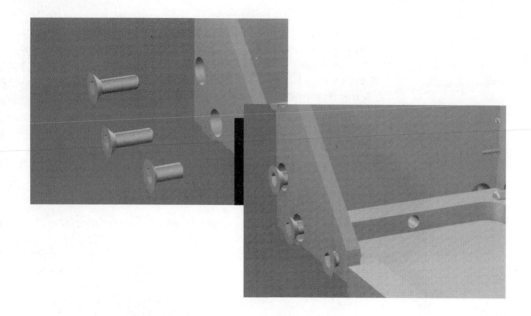

Figure 1-7 ***Parent-Child Relationship in a Hierarchical Link.*** *The movement of the parent fastener causes movement in the children.*

22-1 through 22-3

2-11, 3-42 through 3-46

Autodesk provides a product for this—Animator Studio. Although this workbook doesn't address this software, you should be aware of its capabilities. In Animator Studio, individual animation sequences can be assembled with dramatic transitions. Text, credits, and, with the proper equipment, audio can be added. Finally, Animator Studio files can be output directly to video tape for mass distribution.

1.7 Using the Lab Sheets

Included throughout the chapters in this book are planning and record sheets that are critical for your understanding of the animation process. If you take these sheets seriously, you will produce better animation. Additionally, if you entertain the idea of working professionally in animation, these sheets supplement your actual animation—they let a potential employer know *how* you approach a problem. Sample sheets from a student project are reproduced in this chapter. Study them to see how the project was refined as the sheets were used throughout the entire process.

Using the Lab Sheets

Model Planning Sheet. This sheet (Figure 1-8) provides a space in which to sketch the animation geometry and possibly how camera paths interact with that space. It is this sheet that you will use to plan shapes, lofts, booleans, and primitives. You will use your Model Planning Sheet to guide your constructions. Assign descriptive names to your objects using the balloons.

Animation Storyboard. This sheet is the backbone of an animation. On it, you will identify the *key frames* that control the major position of geometry, cameras, and lights (Figure 1-9). On your storyboard you will *script* the scene in textual form. You will use your Animation Storyboard sheets to place geometry, lights, and cameras as well as put them in motion in the Keyframer Module.

File Organization Sheet. This sheet shows the relationship of individual files as they are assembled to make an animation (Figure 1-10). It is especially important if you ever need to reconstruct which geometry, materials, backgrounds, and texture maps were used in a project. This sheet also allows you to base subsequent animation projects on ones you know to be successful (in other words, you don't have to reinvent the wheel).

Cameras and Lighting Sheet. Record the **RGB*** and **HLS*** values of Ambient, Spot, and Omni lights as well as the color of any background environment used. Also, record the position and target of cameras and lights in X-Y-Z world space as well as focal length and field of view (Figure 1-11).

Objects and Materials Sheet. This sheet (Figure 1-12) records the names of objects used in the animation as well as material assignment and their RGB and HLS values. It provides a way of checking for efficient use of materials.

Frame Planning Sheet. This sheet provides a mechanism for planning the movement and changes in the elements of your animation. Use colors to identify transitions, rotations, scaling, morphing, or other effects. With this sheet (Figure 1-13) you can determine the status of any object in the animation at any frame. This is the core of designing an animation. With this sheet, you are designing. Without this sheet, you are simply playing around.

---

* Several color models are available for describing color. Most illustrators and animators may choose to work in **HLS** (*Hue, Light, Saturation*) when dealing with materials and maps and switch to **RGB** (*Red, Green, Blue*) when specifying lights. The reason for this is that it is difficult to desaturate (add the complement), tint (lighten), or shade (darken) a color in RGB.

1 Introduction

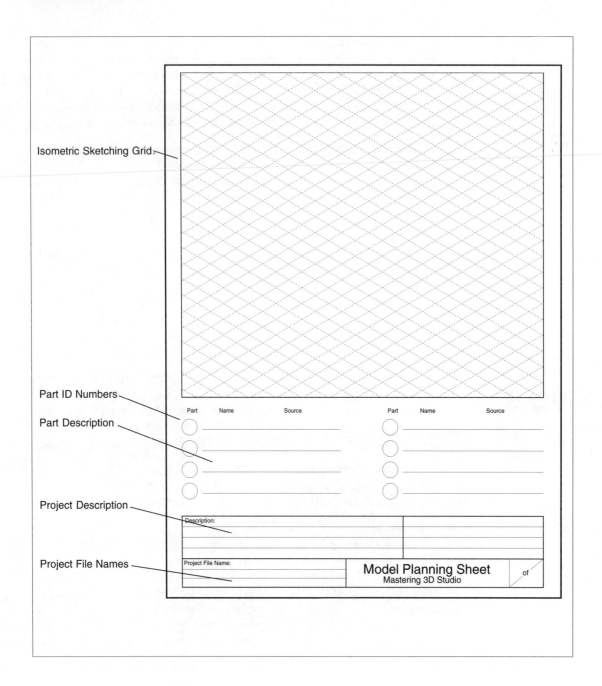

Figure 1-8 **Model Planning Sheet.** *A pictorial sketch helps you make decisions as to which modeling techniques may prove to be most efficient.*

Using the Lab Sheets

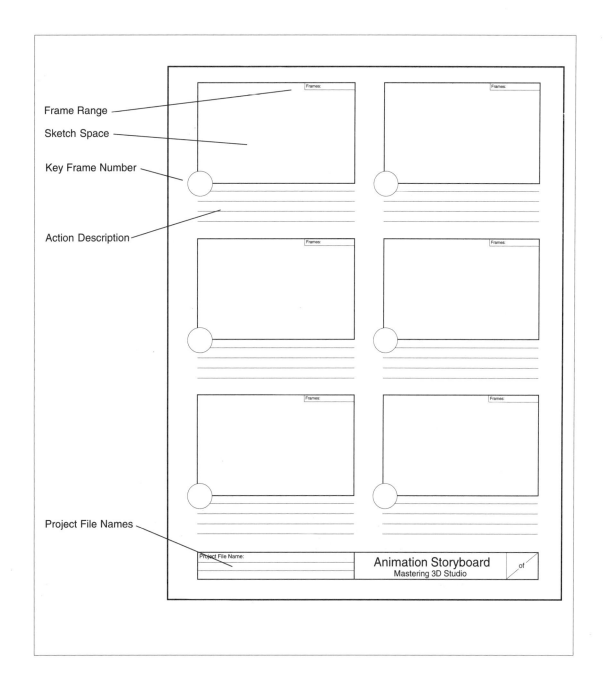

Figure 1-9 **Animation Storyboard.** Sketch key frames on this sheet to help you plan your cameras and lights and their paths. Here you can determine which 3D Studio effects will produce the desired results.

1 Introduction

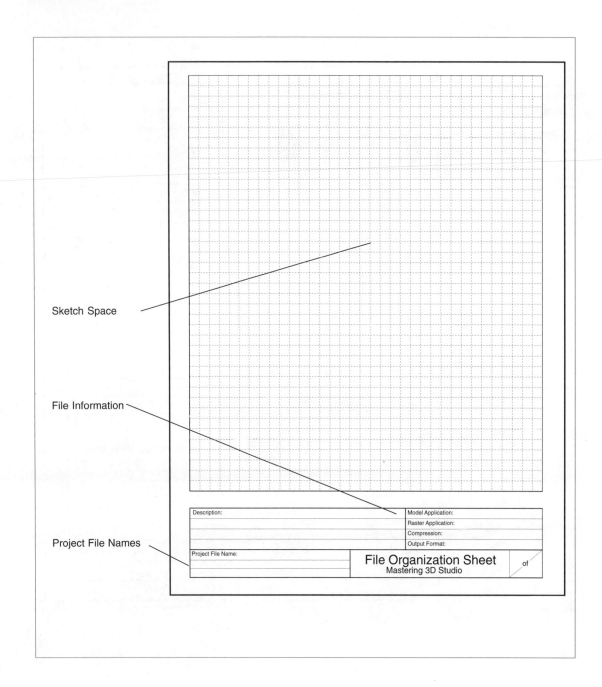

Figure 1-10 **File Organization Sheet.** *Diagram how the pieces of your animation will come together on this sheet. The sources may be 3D Studio, a CAD program, a raster program, or a library of model or materials.*

Using the Lab Sheets

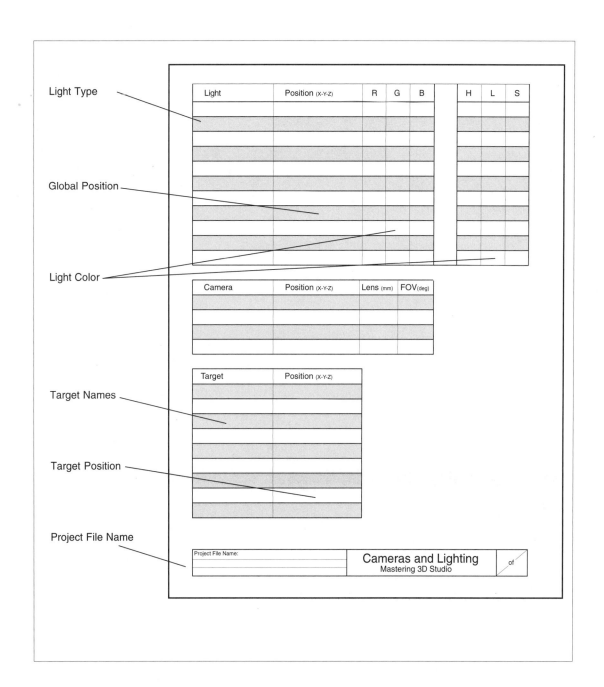

Figure 1-11 **Cameras and Lighting Sheet.** This sheet is completed using the Frame Planning Sheet as a guide. Refer to the settings on this sheet to match cameras and lights in subsequent projects.

1 Introduction

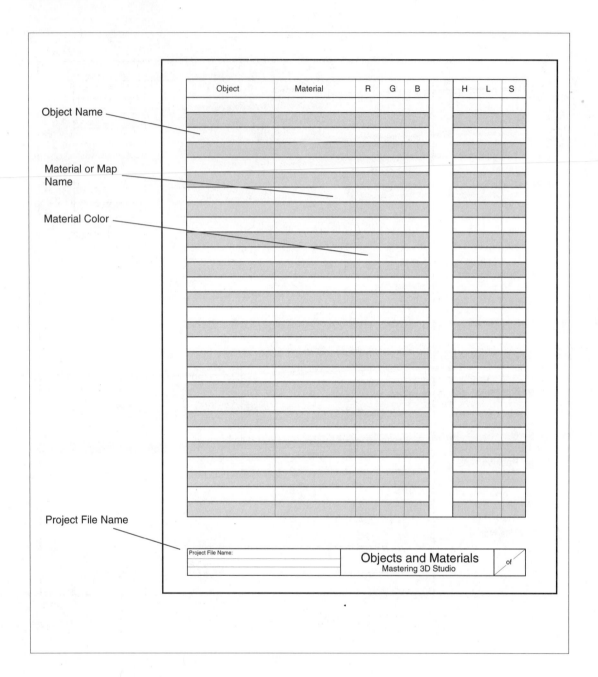

 **Objects and Materials Sheet.** This sheet encourages the efficient use of materials. It allows you to plan object names for use in the 3D Editor. It also provides a record for comparison with other projects so that materials can be reused.

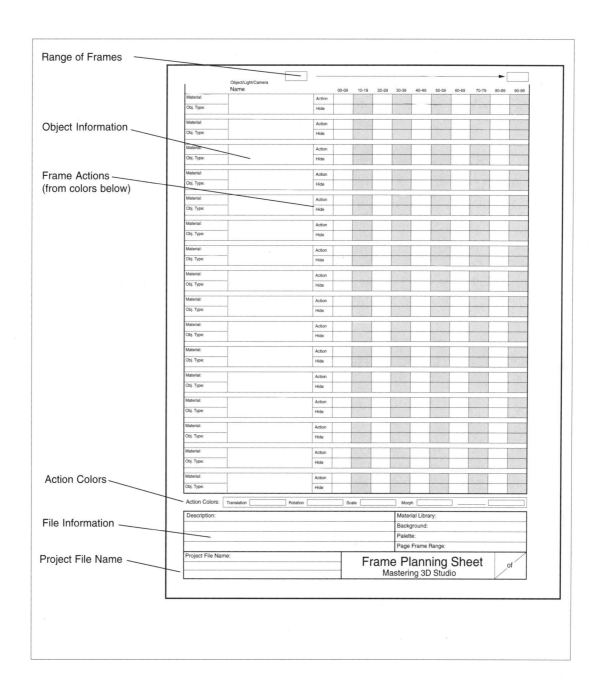

Figure 1-13 **Frame Planning Sheet.** This sheet coordinates the movement of geometry, lights, and cameras. It allows you to determine the state of every object in the animation at any frame.

1.8 Questions to Answer

1. What is the relationship between focal length and depth of field? Does 3D Studio recognize this relationship?

2. How can you tell if a model or image is copyrighted? Put into your own words your understanding of copyright regulations.

3. What is the difference between digital and analog? How does each impact a monitor's ability to display a photorealistically rendered scene?

4. Why must a program like 3D Studio be capable of manipulating both vector and raster data?

5. What is the difference between RGB and HLS color models? When would you use each?

6. Why is animation a process? What control and planning devices are available to monitor and adjust this process?

7. How might you judge the success of an animation? List at least five (5) criteria you might use in evaluation. Be prepared to justify each one.

8. Using a Model Planning Sheet from the back of this book, create a flow chart that describes the animation process from start to finish.

Chapter 2

Modeling

2 Modeling

2.1 Understanding Modeling

It is difficult to overemphasize the importance of modeling in the animation process. In fact, during the course of an animation project you will spend 75% of your time modeling. To be an effective modeler you need to understand both 2D and 3D spatial constructions, you need to understand the applicability of various modeling techniques, and you need to be able to apply the most efficient and effective modeling methods to get the desired results.

An effective modeler knows more than one method of solving a geometric problem. Some shapes are better swept, **lofted**, or booleaned and you must know when to apply each of these techniques. You must also know the characteristics of the software. For example, it would be a waste of time to construct valid and accurate intersections in 3D Studio by tedious editing or **boolean operations** when visibility is automatically determined during rendering. Simply place the objects in correct spatial juxtaposition and let the software determine the intersection at rendering time. Figure 2-1 shows model geometry placed so that intersections are determined during rendering.

What makes an effective model?

Terms to Know and Define

3D Editor Module
boolean operation
bump map
CAD models
camera view
detail (rendering)
DXF format
extruded shape
fundamental shape
geometric precision
global axis system
HOLD
local axis system
lofted shape
Lofter Module
opacity map
primitive shape
Shaper Module
swept shape

1. An effective model has precision appropriate to the task.
Geometry in an animation must be proportionally correct. Large objects (like a house) may require accuracy within an inch or two. Smaller objects viewed up close may require greater accuracy. Small objects when viewed from a distance may not require any detail at all. In most cases, animation accuracy can be less than CAD accuracy. Importing **CAD models** into 3D Studio provides an added benefit of their accuracy, albeit often at the expense of *too much accuracy and detail* to the point where CAD geometry imported into 3D Studio must be edited and simplified to be practicable.

Understanding Modeling

2. *The geometry is created in the correct spatial orientation.* It may be easier to create geometry in a primary position first, and then rotate it into its real position, than to try and create it in an oblique final position. The key is to use an appropriate number of viewports in orientations that make sense for a particular task. Figure 2-2 shows geometry in a typical viewport orientation.

TUTORIAL
3-4, 23-2

REFERENCE
2-5, 3-48

3. *Appropriate construction methods are selected.* As a modeler you should analyze each shape and determine the construction method best suited for its creation. For example, some objects can be created out of 3D Studio's **primitives**. Other geometry lends itself to **extrusion** or is best **swept** using a custom 2D profile. **Boolean operations** add, subtract, and union either primitive shapes or ones you create yourself. Some shapes can be created out of others by scaling them differently in two directions or by translating selected vertices while leaving the rest of the object alone.

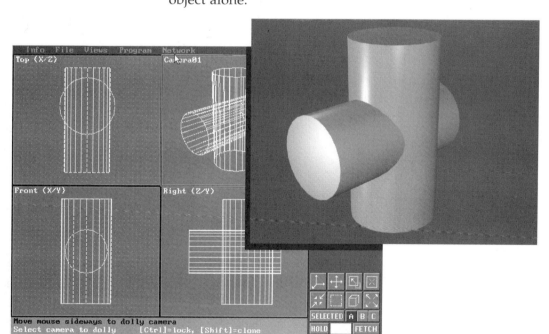

Figure 2-1 **Models Placed in Space.** *Many intersections can be handled by 3D Studio at rendering time, keeping the models simple and rendering times short.*

23

2 Modeling

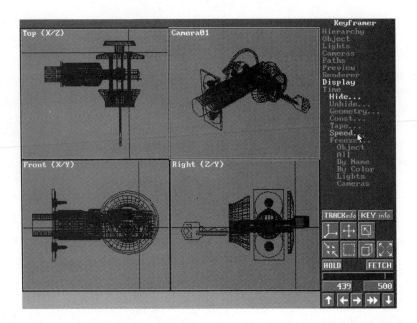

Figure 2-2 **Viewport Orientation.** *The nature of the scene and the geometry within it determines the number and orientation of viewports.*

TUTORIAL
4-1, 4-7

REFERENCE
6-11, 7-127

4. Appropriate surface detail is defined. Knowing how finely divided a surface needs to be in order for the desired effect to be achieved is important. A small sphere, viewed from some distance, may be coarsely defined. A large sphere, viewed from a close distance, would require finer division so that it looks smooth. Knowing surface characteristics ahead of time also helps decide on the necessary level of detail. Surfaces that will be rough or textured can be defined with fewer polygons. Smooth and highly reflective surfaces require smaller divisions.

5. Maps are planned to minimize geometric constructions. Texture, **bump**, and **opacity maps** reduce the need to model geometry. For example, the windshield and side windows of an automobile could be modeled *into* the body or booleaned *out of* the body (Figure 2-3). An opacity map

Understanding Modeling

with the opacity set at zero would result in transparency *at rendering time*. Tire treads could be cut into a tire profile by subtracting the tread shape or by positioning tread blocks on the outside of a cylinder but this would be a tedious process and result in object geometry of great complexity. Instead, a bump map with the bump set to an appropriate number of pixels would produce treads *at rendering time*.

6. *The model is saved in an appropriate format.* If the model is created outside 3D Studio, it must be saved in a format that 3D Studio recognizes. This is typically AutoCAD's **DXF format**. Most popular CAD software includes DXF as an export option. Your Student Edition limits rendering to 256 colors, which is sufficient for display on most color monitors that have this limitation.

REFERENCE
3-36, 3-42 through 3-45

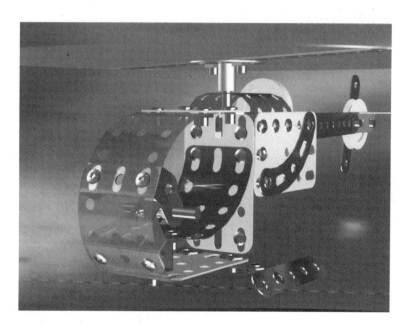

Figure 2-3 **Using Maps to Simplify Modeling.** *The use of a map to create transparency not only simplifies the model but allows alternatives to be entertained on the same base geometry.*

25

2.2 You Must Know Space

To effectively use 3D Studio's modeling tools, you must be comfortable in navigating around in 3D space. True, many of the constructions will be started in the **Shaper Module** where 2D profiles are defined, but knowing how those profiles eventually will be turned into 3D shapes determines how the shape is lofted and where it is placed in the **3D Editor**.

A key to operating in 3D space is to arrange an appropriate number of views in the Editor. This necessitates mentally moving from plan, elevation, profile, and pictorial views and all the time translating coordinate directions from view to view.

Efficient use of spatial directions involves:

3-24, 21-22

5-11, 6-4

1. Planning the position of geometric elements relative to the global axis system. Place an identifiable feature of the scene at the **global axis system** origin (0,0,0) of the workspace. This makes constructions simple because coordinate numbers are manageable. Plus, if the geometry is symmetrical, constructions are further simplified.

2. Using the local axis system to simplify constructions. When geometry doesn't adhere to the global system, a **local axis system** can be used. This approach makes more sense than attempting to calculate coordinate positions relative to the global axis system by means of trigonometry.

3. Setting cameras to yield views for which a local axis system makes sense. Having a local axis feature works only if you can match the coordinate directions with the desired features on geometry. Camera position determines how global and local axis directions relate to features on an object. **Camera view** is especially important in angular or oblique constructions.

2.3 Approaches to Modeling

There is no one best approach to modeling. Each object, by its very nature, may require a totally different approach. It is your task to analyze geometry and determine which modeling method produces the best results in the most efficient manner. The best way to do this is to take a low-tech approach. SKETCH! In sketching out a modeling solution you make decisions off the computer. It makes you more productive when you work in 3D Studio. It is much easier to abandon a sketch that took you five minutes than a computer model that took you five hours. We have provided Model Planning Sheets to help you with this task.

A general guideline—in both sketching and 3D Studio—is to work from the general to the specific. That is, *macro model* first. Assemble large volumes that don't have much detail to test the feasibility of the model. You may be able to satisfy the requirements of the problem without resorting to *micro modeling*.

Readings

Tutorial   Tutorial 3, 4, & 8

Reference Chapters 5, 6, & 7
Define the terms on page 22.

2 Modeling

2.4 Use Predefined Primitives

The primitives of Box, Sphere, Hemisphere, Cylinder, Torus, and Cone can be scaled differently in X, Y, and Z directions and combined spatially to create almost any general shape. Try this method first. Then, you can adjust individual vertices to further refine the shape (Figure 2-4).

TUTORIAL
8-1 through 8-4

REFERENCE
7-19 through 7-23

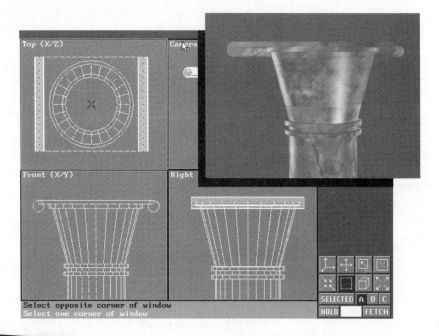

Figure 2-4 *Using Primitives in Modeling.* Very satisfactory results can be obtained by using scaled primitives as shown in this example.

2.5 Create a Profile

TUTORIAL
3-1 through 3-10

REFERENCE
5-1 through 5-10

The 2D Shaper creates a profile in the X-Y plane. The shape can become the basis of a user-created object that is treated like one of the shape primitives. Because many 3D objects are represented as 2D views in engineering and technical drawings, these views often form the basis for the shape. A quick sketch can often determine the **fundamental shape**. The fundamental shape is devoid of **detail** and functions as a primitive (Figure 2-5).

28

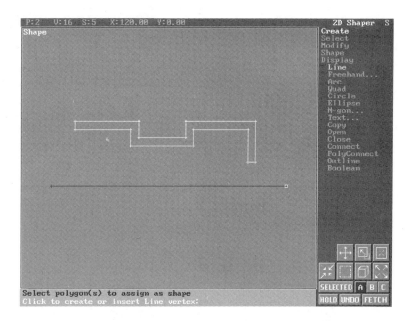

Figure 2-5 ...pe in the Shaper Module. Careful analysis of an object's shape can lead to effective extrusions and sweeps.

2.6   Create a Lofted Extrusion

4-1 through 4-15

6-1 through 6-13

Because a shape is strictly a 2D object, making something meaningful out of it requires the addition of Z or depth information. The 3D **Lofter Module** in 3D Studio accepts a shape from the Shaper and manipulates that shape along a path. You determine the nature of the path. If the path is linear, the loft can be thought of as an extrusion. Many things can be done to the shape as it is translated along the path. It can be repeated, scaled, rotated, flipped, or combined with other shapes in a boolean-like combination. Figure 2-6 shows the shape from the previous figure **extruded** and swept.

2.7 Create a Swept Shape

REFERENCE
6-25

A 2D shape lofted along a closed path (often a circle) results in a **swept shape** or surface of revolution. This is done in the 2D Lofter. Swept shapes have symmetrical cross sections. Of course, the closed shape can be any shape. A tube can be a circle lofted along an irregular curved path. Figure 2-7 shows the shape from the last two figures swept in a circular path.

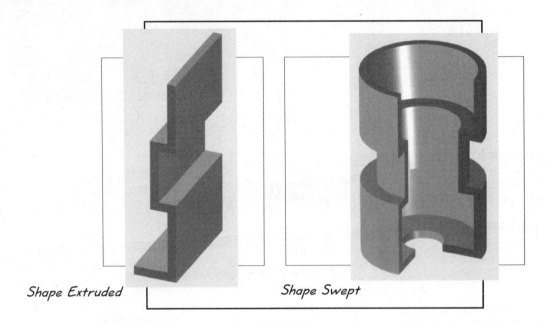

Shape Extruded   Shape Swept

Figure 2-6 *Shape in the Lofter Module. Note how the same shape will produce entirely different results when it extrudes or sweeps along or around a path.*

2.8 Boolean Union

TUTORIAL
7-5 through 7-9
23-2 through 23-6

REFERENCE
6-72 through 6-76
7-54 through 7-56

Boolean operations are performed in the 3D Editor. When two objects are unioned, all material belonging to the two individual objects is included in the resulting product. It makes no difference in which order the two objects are identified. In 3D Studio you can often avoid boolean operations for simple intersections

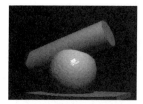

Union

Subtraction

Intersection

because the rendering engine will determine how objects come together when making the rendering. Avoiding booleans also keeps geometry tessellation simpler, a benefit when assigning materials and during editing. Also, don't think that unioning objects is the only method or for that matter the best way of treating several objects as a unit.

Perform boolean union when an additional operation, such as subtraction, must cross the two shapes, making valid interior surfaces. Figure 2-8 shows a boolean union of our familiar geometry with a primitive.

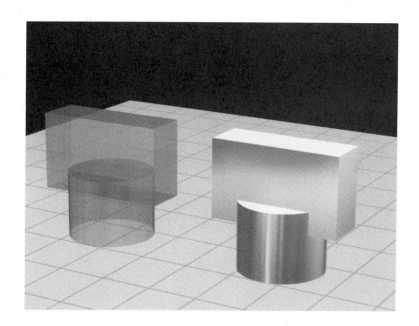

Figure 2-7 *Boolean Union. This operation creates a new object that includes all surfaces of each. Surfaces inside the union are removed.*

2.9 Boolean Subtraction

Boolean subtraction can often be the best way to achieve complex profiles. Think of this operation as tool-based. That is, think of one object (the tool) as removing its shape from another object (the material). The result of this operation depends on which object is the tool and which is the material. Switch the two and you'll get completely different results(Figure 2-9). For this reason, you may want to start a library of shapes and lofts that can be used as tools. Boolean operations are not perfect, especially when you inadvertently choose shapes whose ends unfortunately align perfectly. Always provide for more tool than is necessary to fully intersect the material. Still, unpredictable results may occur and the visibility of planes will not be correctly resolved. Always **HOLD** the current state of the 3D Editor before performing boolean operations.

An alternative to a boolean subtraction may be to apply a bump map and allow the 3D Studio rendering engine to create subtle contours at rendering time. This would be preferable in the case of grooves, joints, treads, or tiles.

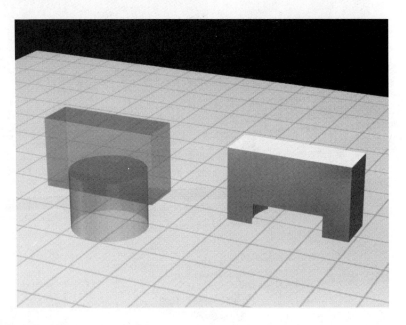

Figure 2-8 **Boolean Subtraction.** *Where a union isn't sensitive to the order of operation, subtraction results will vary depending on object order.*

2.10 Boolean Intersection

The intersection operation is possibly the most powerful and the most difficult-to-understand boolean. In an intersection, only material common to the two shapes is kept while material outside the intersection is discarded. This procedure can be accomplished in two ways in 3D Studio. First, in the 2D Lofter, polygons can be fitted together forming a "double extrusion." This results in very usable primitive shapes. The second way is to use the intersect boolean function in the 3D Editor. The latter is more flexible.

Boolean intersection is appropriate for objects for which profiles are readily identifiable. For example, if you can easily create the top, front, and side profiles of a complex shape—a boat hull, for example—the compound surface of the boat is two boolean intersections operations away. The first operation might intersect top and front profiles. The second might intersect the side profile with the result of the first intersection. The results can be quite striking (Figure 2-10).

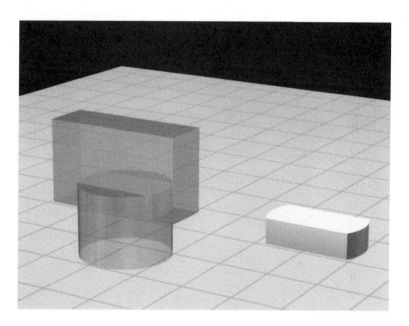

Figure 2-9 **Boolean Intersection.** *Complex geometries can be formed by intersecting primitive shapes.*

2.11 CAD Models

3D Studio readily accepts DXF files from AutoCAD or other products. Two-dimensional DXF shapes can be brought into the 2D Shaper or 3D Lofter. Entire 3D DXF surface models can be brought into the 3D Editor. The validity of these models depends

2 Modeling

20-2

2-12, 3-19, 3-36

on how they were constructed in the CAD software. It isn't uncommon to spend considerable time in 3D Studio editing CAD data so that you can assign materials and maps. Remember, CAD data is used for entirely different purposes than rendering and animation. Figure 2-11 shows the development of a model that was started in AutoCAD, brought into 3D Studio as a DXF file, and combined there with 3D Studio's modeling tools to produce a photorealistically rendered scene.

It is entirely appropriate to model in a CAD environment and bring the geometry into 3D Studio. However, for most technical animations, the level of precision indigenous to CAD models far exceeds that required in 3D Studio and may actually negatively impact development time. (You may have a CAD tool that writes less than optimum DXF files resulting in spurious results in 3D Studio.) In any case, consider the following when deciding whether to uses existing CAD data:

1. If you have access to engineering data, either 2D or 3D, in good DXF format, by all means use it.

2. If you have to create model geometry that will be used in other engineering functions (analysis, tool path generation, documentation), use a CAD tool and import the results into 3D Studio.

3. If your geometry will be used for rendering or animation exclusively, create the geometry directly in 3D Studio.

2.12 Modeling Exercises

On the following pages are exercises that develop both modeling and sketching skills. They make use of extrusion, sweeping, and boolean operations. Use a soft pencil and perform all lettering in a style approved by your instructor.

Modeling Exercises

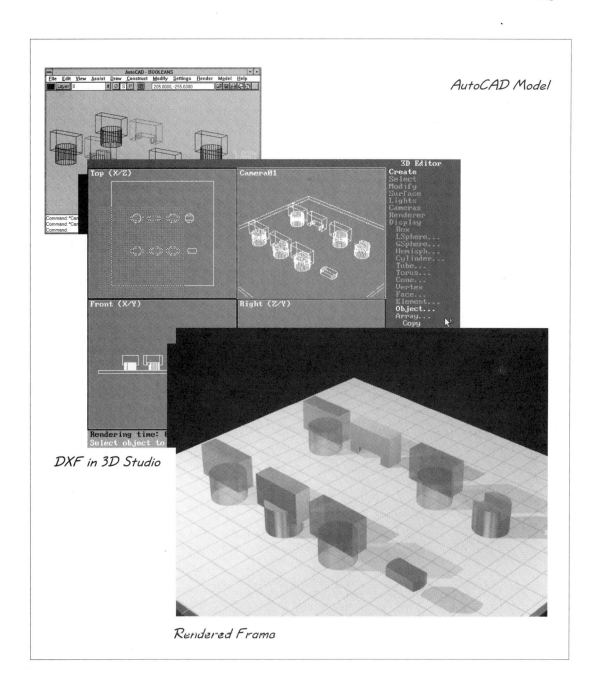

Figure 2-10 Using CAD Data.

2.13 Questions to Answer

1. Discuss a negative factor in using model geometry directly from a CAD system.

2. Why is it important to create model geometry at rendeing time by using bump or opacity maps? Describe how each works.

3. Consider the following objects: a tire, a hose, a wheelbarrow, and a knurled knob. Describe the sequence of modeling and mapping you would use to create the part.

4. Describe the three modeling modules available in 3D Studio. How can geometry be brought into each? How, and why, is geometry taken out of each module.

5. Choose a complex *organic* object. Use a Model Planning Sheet from the back of this book to explore how it might be modeled in 3D Studio. Try to think of the simplest (and possibly most obvious) solution first.

Extrude the profiles and determine the resulting intersection.

Sweep the profile about the circular path. Box out the general form first. Then complete cylinders, add detail, and determine visibility.

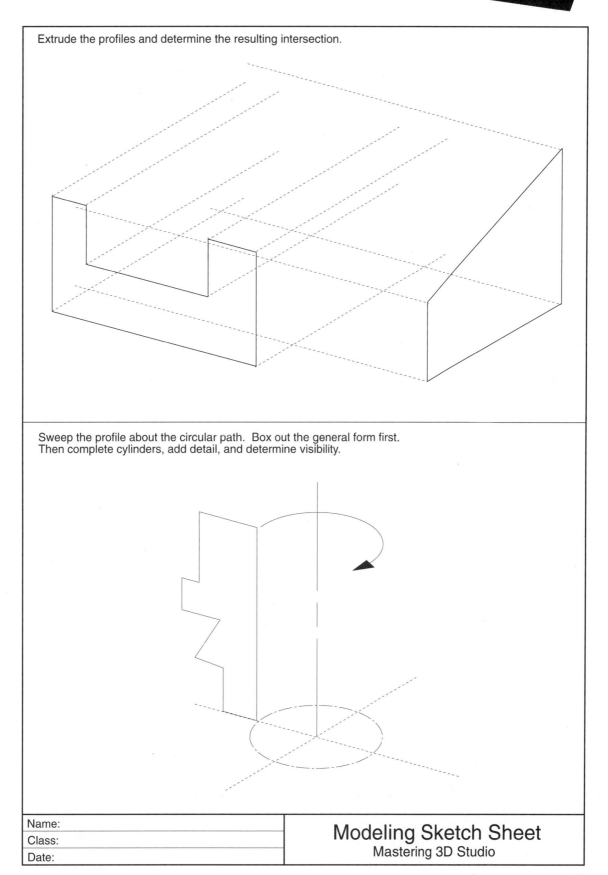

Name:
Class:
Date:

Modeling Sketch Sheet
Mastering 3D Studio

Modeling Worksheet

Based on the overlapping solid primitives shown below and the Boolean operations assigned, darken all visible edges of the resulting composite solid as shown in the following examples. Your instructor may choose to assign one or more operations to each of the four problems.

UNION (A+B)　　DIFFERENCE (A-B)　　DIFFERENCE (B-A)　　INTERSECTION (A∩B)

1　○ UNION (A+B)　　○ DIFFERENCE (A-B)
　　○ INTERSECTION (A∩B)　　○ DIFFERENCE (B-A)

2　○ UNION (A+B)　　○ DIFFERENCE (A-B)
　　○ INTERSECTION (A∩B)　　○ DIFFERENCE (B-A)

3　○ UNION (A+B)　　○ DIFFERENCE (A-B)
　　○ INTERSECTION (A∩B)　　○ DIFFERENCE (B-A)

4　○ UNION (A+B)　　○ DIFFERENCE (A-B)
　　○ INTERSECTION (A∩B)　　○ DIFFERENCE (B-A)

Name:
Class:
Date:

Modeling Sketch Sheet
Mastering 3D Studio

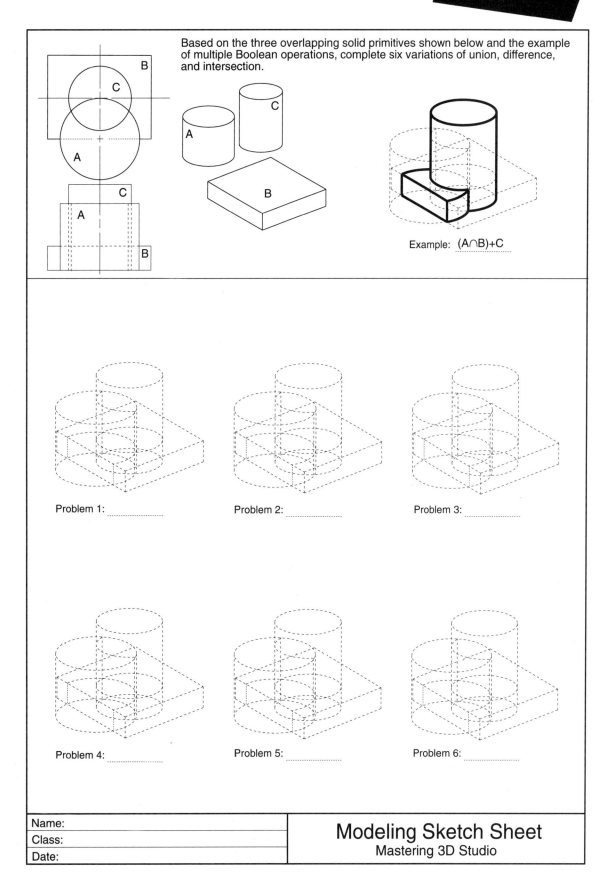

Based on the three overlapping solid primitives shown below and the example of multiple Boolean operations, complete six variations of union, difference, and intersection.

Example: $(A \cap B)+C$

Problem 1: _____ Problem 2: _____ Problem 3: _____

Problem 4: _____ Problem 5: _____ Problem 6: _____

Name:
Class:
Date:

Modeling Sketch Sheet
Mastering 3D Studio

Chapter 3

Rendering

3 Rendering

3.1 Understanding Rendering

A rendering is an abstraction of a real-world or hypothetical situation done in a particular medium. You can have pencil renderings, watercolor renderings, airbrush renderings, and, yes, digital computer renderings. Each medium is best suited to certain applications. For example, an *airbrush rendering* is effective for highly reflective objects or objects that require extremely smooth transitions. An *acrylic rendering* is effective when there are fewer smooth transitions. A *marker rendering* is appropriate for material that has streaks, like wood grain. Choosing the best medium for a particular object is the first step in rendering. A rendering that is only slightly abstracted from what one would expect to see in a lifelike situation is called a **photorealistic rendering**.

Figure 3-1 shows a sequence of renderings in which realism increases with each frame. In the final frame, the image appears to be a photograph of a real object.

Electronic graphics places an almost unlimited number of rendering tools and effects in the hands of an illustrator or animator. You can make a rendering look smooth, streaky, like a collection of dots, or featuring brush marks or watercolor blends. These effects are often called **filters**.

The heart of every animation is a series of effectively rendered still frames. If poor rendering decisions are made, it almost assuredly will result in a poor animation. However, because an animation depends on several factors other than rendering—cameras and the temporal factors of motion—well-rendered frames *don't guarantee* an effective animation. An added benefit from animation is having access to a large number of still frames that can be used in traditional publishing.

What makes an effective rendering?

> **1. An effective rendering is based on correct geometry.** In a technical rendering, the accuracy of the underlying geometry is all-important. If the geometry is wrong, decisions made about the efficacy of the subject—such as "Are we going to commit several million dollars to this project?"—may be wrong.

Terms to Know and Define

ambient light
bit depth
data bus
environment map
filters
materials
native format
omni light
photorealistic
   rendering
rendering cues
rendering modes
resolution
spot light
texture

Understanding Rendering

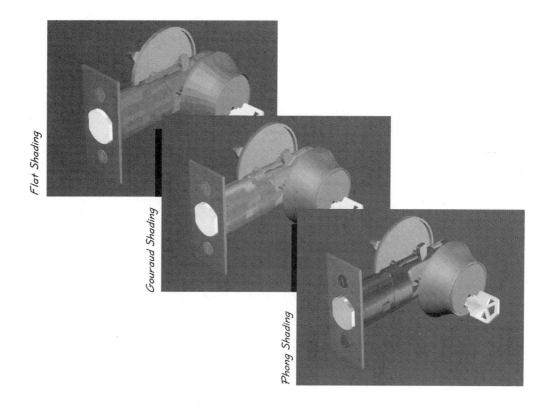

Figure 3-1 *Increasing Photorealism. Your choice of materials and lighting, along with the rendering mode used, control the level of photorealism.*

1-17, 20-14

7-181, 7-217

2. The geometry is displayed in an effective orientation. If a product is generally seen, used, or identified from a certain vantage or in a certain orientation, it would be unwise (and generally ineffective) to place the object in some obscure position to be viewed from a bizarre vantage point. Look at the familiar object in Figure 3-2. Which view would be more effective in purchasing, installation, or maintenance?

3. Appropriate and effective materials are applied. The materials chosen must render realistically. This may be a circular proposition, one best served by experience. Knowledge that a material will appear a certain way when output to the screen, to videotape, or to one of a dozen digital printing technologies reduces the need for time-consuming proofs. Applying a marble **texture** (because

3 Rendering

you can) to an object that is normally matte plastic is not effective rendering.

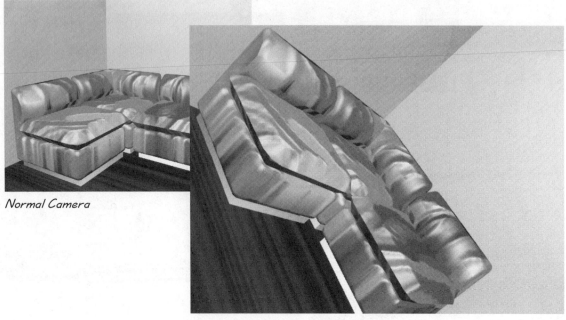

Normal Camera

Camera Roll Adjusted

 Realistic Camera Angles. *Realism is enhanced by wise choice of camera position, focal length, and field of view. In the second frame, camera roll has been adjusted.*

4. Effective lighting is chosen. Having access to unlimited lighting sources is not a positive feature; it almost always leads to over-lighting a scene. Almost all effective renderings include the following:

- One strong main source of natural light.

- One secondary reflected light source of blue or red.

- One soft tertiary light source to provide back lighting.

Figure 3-3 shows both ineffective and effective lighting. In the first example, strong **ambient light** fills in all shade and shadows created by **spot lights** set too far away.

Understanding Rendering

Figure 3-3 *Effect of Strong Ambient Light.* Strong ambient light has a tendency to negate shades and shadows and make a scene appear less realistic.

5. Intelligent filters are used. Filters can be used to create special effects at rendering time, such as embossing, pointilizing, and adding atmospheric haze, motion, or blur, just to name a few. The strength of using filters is that some effects can be achieved by this technique that would be tedious or impossible if attempted in the model.

6. The rendering is created at an appropriate resolution. **Resolution** is a function of the number of pixels horizontally and vertically (say, 640 x 480) and the depth of information at each pixel (say, 8-bits or 256 colors). This again depends somewhat on experience. Rendering at too course a resolution may result in a grainy, pixelated image. Rendering at too high a resolution results in a file larger (in terms of required storage and display memory) than necessary.

3 Rendering

Use these rules of thumb in determining output resolution:

- Render at a resolution that matches your target output device. If the rendering will be displayed on a 72 dot-per-inch 8-bit video monitor, the resolution of the rendering should be 72 dots per inch and 8 bits.

- Render at the lowest resolution necessary to accomplish the task.

- Render at the highest resolution *if the intended use of the rendering is unknown*. You can always go back and create a lower resolution image if need be.

REFERENCE
3-43 through 3-45

7. The rendering is saved in an appropriate format. It is important to understand that model geometry is created and saved as *objects* or *vectors*. The rendering is a *raster* or *bit-map* rendition based on the choice of materials, lights, filters, and cameras.

- Save the geometry in the **native format** of the application first.

- Save the raster rendering in formats appropriate for the intended output.

Readings

Tutorial	Tutorials 9, 10, & 11
Reference	Chapter 7, pages 7-172 through 7-217

48

3.2 Influence of Light Sources

In a rendering, intelligent choice of light source makes the subject matter come alive. The lighting scheme should reflect how the subject is being viewed. Interior objects hardly ever are illuminated by single, intense, directly focused light sources. Most interior objects cast diffused shadows and have reflected light—usually natural blue light from a window. Exterior objects are influenced by time of day (angle and hue of light), and reflected light from grass, ground, or pavement. Consider the following when making decisions concerning lighting:

REFERENCE

7-153, 7-169, 7-198

1. The light must be the correct intensity. Without sufficient light, a rendering will appear dim and dark. With too much light, surface characteristics and geometric features will be washed out. With the correct *amount* of light, sunlight, shade, and shadow will accurately reveal the object's geometric shape (Figure 3-4).

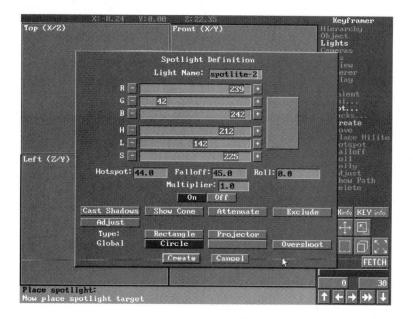

Figure 3-4 **Lighting Options.** *This dialogue box provides controls for each light object in your scene.*

3 Rendering

13-3, 13-11

2. The light must be at an appropriate angle. Take into account both the viewing direction and the geometric features on the object. Very seldom would you want to light a scene from directly behind the viewer. Neither would you place a primary light source directly in front of the viewer (Figure 3-5).

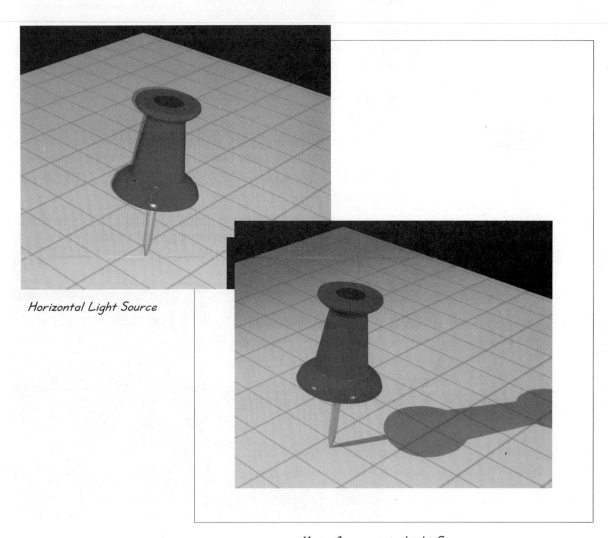

Horizontal Light Source

More Appropriate Light Source

Figure 3-5 **Common Lighting Mistake.** *In the first example, light sources are too horizontal. In the second example, lights are directed at the subject from above and behind the camera.*

Influence of Light Sources

7-147 through 7-160

3. Lights must be of an appropriate type. You have several types of lights available to light a scene. Ambient light, spot lights, and **omni lights** all possess their own characteristics. Effective lighting combines these so that objects in the scene are realistic and understandable (Figure 3-6). For example, important detail is not obscured by heavy shadows or extensive highlights.

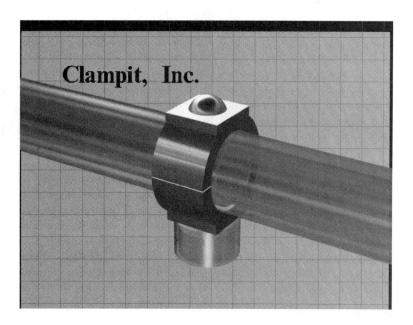

Figure 3-6 **Light Source Types.** *This scene uses ambient, omni, and spot lights.*

51

4. Secondary lights must enhance shape or environment.
Every light must have a purpose and add to a scene. The best lighting strategy is a minimalist strategy: Use the fewest number of lights necessary to achieve the desired results. Note in Figure 3-7 that a light illuminating a rear surface allows the shape of a dark subject to be easily seen.

Figure 3-7 **Backlighting.** *Because a dark object will not show dramatic sun, shade, and shadow, illuminate a surface behind the object to show contrast and shape.*

3.3 Importance of Materials

If lighting makes a scene come alive, effective **materials** make the difference in whether or not a scene is realistic. Wood *must* look like wood. Chrome *must* look like chrome. Stucco *must* look like stucco. If they don't, you won't have a realistic rendering.

Material maps are raster images. They are a collection of dots that, when viewed from a known distance, give the *appearance* of a material. To create your own materials, you must use a raster

Importance of Materials

TUTORIAL
10-1 through 10-28

REFERENCE
9-1 through 9-6

editor like the Materials Editor supplied with 3D Studio. You can, however, use any raster image processor such as Photoshop™ or Fractel Painter™ as long as the material can be saved in a format 3D Studio recognizes. If you are serious about creating your own materials, these products offer greater flexibility and powerful filters for achieving creative results. Figure 3-8 shows several materials created in a raster program.

If you want realism, there's nothing like capturing a picture of the material. The easiest way to do this is to take a snapshot with a digital camera or capture an image with a video camera and appropriate software. You may still have to edit or tweak the image even though it's a picture of a real material. Figure 3-9 shows several materials from direct video capture.

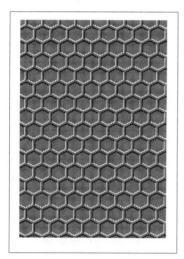

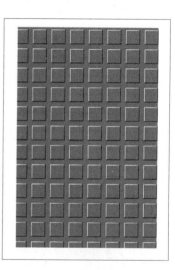

Figure 3-8 **Raster Materials.** *These materials were created in a raster painting program for use in 3D Studio.*

The following are considerations in planning material choices:

1. Materials must be realistic at output resolution. This is very important. A material's detail (like wood grain, bumps, pits, grooves, etc.) can disappear altogether at distance and appear rough and pixelated up close.

3 Rendering

Figure 3-9 **Materials From Video Capture.** *Capturing video frames in raster format is an inexpensive and realistic way to get materials into 3D Studio.*

11-1 through 11-22

7-137 through 7-139

2. Materials must be mapped to objects realistically.
Materials must be properly aligned, scaled, and applied to surfaces for photorealistic results. Planar, cylindrical, and spherical maps can be applied to a variety of surfaces, achieving different results. Creative results can often be achieved by intentionally mismatching map and surface geometries.

3. Combine material and bump maps for realistic results. A realistic picture of wood grain is made even more realistic by combining the wood material with a matching bump map. The material map gives the surface its color and the bump map its surface deviations or perturbations.

3.4 Material Maps

A map is a raster image that represents some characteristic of the surface. A *material map* creates the visual impression of the surface's color—in sunlight, shade, and shadow. A *bump map* is a black-white-gray overlay that tells the rendering engine which pixels of the material map are above or below its nominal surface. A texture map combines material and bump procedures. An opacity map tells the rendering engine which pixels to treat as transparent and which to treat as opaque (the color of the material and the texture of the bump) and all the possibilities in between. An **environment map** produces the illusion of an environment around the scene by mapping a picture of the surrounding panorama to reflective surfaces.

3.5 Detail! Detail! Detail!

Your attention to detail in both modeling and rendering can often spell the difference between an effective rendering (and subsequent animation) and a disaster. Effective detail can be encouraged when you practice the following:

> *1. Include detail that makes a difference.* Don't waste your time with detail that will be indistinguishable at viewing distance. Don't include detail that will be lost because of the angle of view or the position of light sources. Don't include detail smaller that the resolution of the final rendering. For example, if the final rendering will be done at 1200 dpi, nothing smaller than .0008 of an inch on the final output will be discernible.

> *2. Include detail that characterizes the subject.* Does the object have identifying text, trim, manufacturing, or construction details? Some objects are identified by specific details. Omit these and the very nature of the object is lost. Figure 3-10 shows a product without and with its detail. Which looks more realistic to you?

3 Rendering

Figure 3-10 *Importance of Detail.* Compare these two rendered frames. You can see the importance of detail in a realistic rendering.

3.6 Environment

TUTORIAL
9-19 through 9-23

REFERENCE
7-192 through 7-200

The environment is the world around your rendering. Objects outdoors are surrounded by sky, horizon, and ground. Failure to include these elements behind your outdoor scene, or reflected into your scene if you have reflective materials, results in an ineffective rendering. Objects indoors are surrounded by walls, floors, ceilings, lights, and windows (with or without an outdoor environment). Failure to include these elements around and in your indoor scene results in a less than effective rendering.

One of the most effective techniques is to map an environment to the inside of a shape such as a cylinder or hemisphere. This is especially effective when camera angles change in elevation. Keep the diameter of the cylinder or sphere sufficiently large and use a strong omni light to evenly illuminate the background. Figure 3-11 shows an architectural subject with a spherical environment map in its construction and rendered forms.

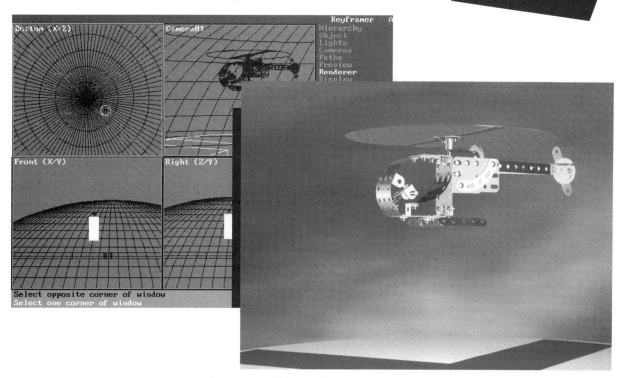

Figure 3-11 ***Background Mapped to a Surface.*** *Note how the consistent lighting and focus gives the background a realistic effect.*

3.7 Rendering Cues

There are several **rendering cues** that make an image look more realistic.

> ***1. Values are never consistent over a surface.*** Because light sources diffuse light over a distance, a surface will hardly ever be evenly illuminated. The larger the surface, the greater the illumination change. Multiple light sources have the tendency to even out the light.
>
> ***2. Shadows will hardly ever be sharp edged.*** Only in extreme lighting conditions will shadows produce a sharp edge. The more distant the light source and the more sources of secondary and reflected light, the softer will be the shadows.

3. Hues will become lighter and bluer as they recede into the distance. This gradation allows the perception of depth without perspective convergence or overlap. Combined with convergence and overlap, hue change can be a dramatic way to add layers of depth to your rendering.

3.8 Photorealistic Rendering

Colorplate Samples

Having access to electronic rendering tools does not lessen the importance of making intelligent rendering decisions. A rendering engine, like 3D Studio, will render any scene you create using the modeling, mapping, lighting, and viewing parameters you establish. If you make less than optimum decisions, 3D Studio will create a less than optimum rendering. Your responsibility is to assure, through your understanding of general rendering properties and the capabilities of the software, that the result is an effective rendering. After the computer has finished the rendering you should be able to evaluate the image in terms of the considerations mentioned in this chapter. You must be able to adjust geometry position, mapping, camera, and lights to produce an effective image.

To make good decisions about the effectiveness of a rendering requires a careful matching of hardware and software. Following is a little tech talk. To observe the full capabilities of 3D Studio's powerful rendering engine, you must have a video board capable of calculating a minimum of 24 bits of color information per screen pixel with enough video memory to display the colors at a minimum resolution of 640 x 480. You must have a video monitor capable of displaying the colors at the desired resolution. You must have a CPU capable of calculating the position of the pixels in an acceptable amount of time. Finally, you must have a **data bus** of sufficient width (32 or 64 bits wide) to be able to push the data between the CPU and the monitor or storage device quickly enough to yield acceptable rendering times. If you have less than these capabilities, you must accept rendering limitations.

It is a temptation to render a scene to the screen at the earliest possible moment at high resolution using the most sophisticated rendering algorithm. As **rendering modes** increase in realism, more and more calculations are required, extending the time required to compute and display the scene. Use the following considerations when rendering a scene:

1. In the construction stage, always render in wire mode. It allows you to concentrate on the geometry. It also has the smallest penalty in terms of the time required to determine and display the rendered image (Figure 3-12).

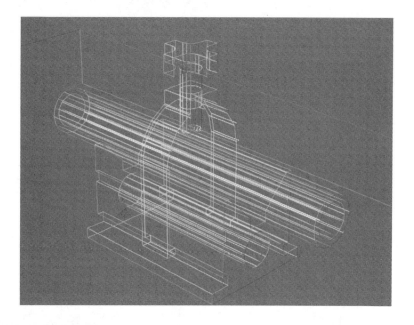

Figure 3-12 **Wire Frame Rendering.** Use this mode during construction.

2. Once the geometry is completed, render in flat mode. This is your first check on surface validity. It is useful in determining whether lights have been set appropriately for the desired results. No shadows are cast, but the position, scale, and appropriateness of textures can be determined (Figure 3-13).

3 Rendering

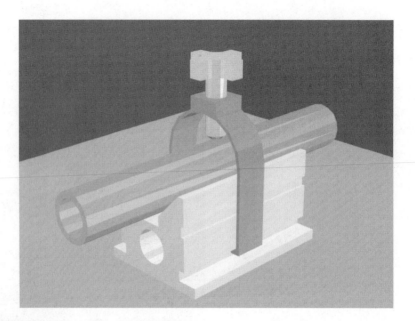

Figure 3-13 **Flat Shading.** Use this rendering mode to test the validity of surfaces and intersections before material assignments.

3. If you don't have cast shadows, opacity, or bump maps, use the Gouraud mode for your final output. This mode is appropriate for objects consisting of soft, matte materials on relatively smooth surfaces (Figure 3-14).

REFERENCE
8-116 through 8-119

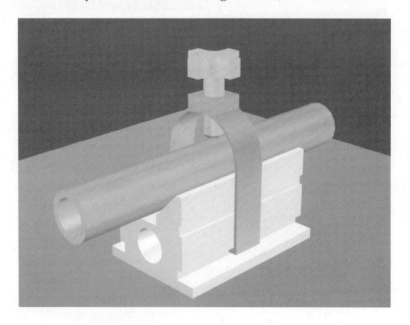

Figure 3-14 **Gouraud Shading.** Use this rendering mode with nonreflective materials or when shadows are not being cast.

4. Reserve the Phong mode for scenes containing cast shadows, texture or bump maps, opacity maps, and reflections. Because of the power of this rendering technique, mistakes in surface geometry, mapping, and lighting can often be exacerbated (Figure 3-15).

5. Choose color palette carefully. Render with a palette, at a resolution, at a **bit depth**, and in a file format appropriate for the intended use. It doesn't do any good to specify a resolution and bit depth (number of colors) that you are unable to calculate because of a limited video adapter. Likewise, rendering to a file format unsuited to the intended use is counterproductive. Determine the appropriate format for video display, process printing separation, and direct output to video tape.

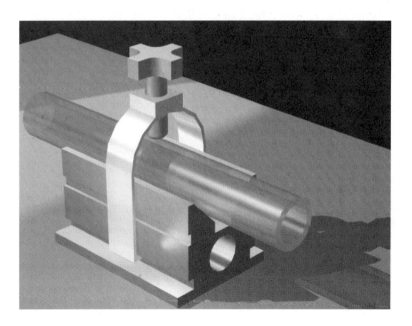

Figure 3-15 *Phong Shading. This most realistic rendering mode is capable of casting shadows, creating reflections, and using bump, texture, and opacity maps.*

6. Make efficient use of your time. Render scenes during periods that can be used productively for other purposes. You can open mail, clean up your work space, go to lunch, or—in the case of rendering a highly detailed and complicated scene with extensive maps and lights—go home and

3 Rendering

let the computer render overnight or over the weekend. Your teacher (and ultimately your boss) isn't interested in having you sit in front of the computer watching it render a scene to disk or the screen.

3.9 Rendering Exercises

Several sheets have been provided at the end of this chapter for you to practice basic sketching and rendering skills. These exercises accomplish two goals: They further hone your sketching skills, skills that are important for storyboards, and they help develop an understanding of what a scene will look like when rendered *before* computer rendering.

3.10 Questions to Answer

1. Discuss the relationship between the ability of 3D Studio to calculate a range of colors and your ability to see these colors on the screen.

2. What rendering mode is necessary to make cast shadows?

3. Describe the differences between the three types of lighting sources and how each is used.

4. What are the methods available for creating realistic material maps?

6. Define the following types of maps and describe in technical terms how each works: material, bump, texture, and opacity.

7. What are the native formats available for saving work in 3D Studio?

8. What is the relationship between data bandwidth and efficient rendering. Where may bottlenecks develop?

Based on the direction of light as represented by the arrow, render the following forms. Assume the objects are resting on a horizontal surface. Use the pole example to estimate shadow lengths. Show sun, shade, and shadow.

Example:

Name:	**Rendering Sketch Sheet**
Class:	Mastering 3D Studio
Date:	

Rendering Worksheets

Rendering Worksheets

Based on the direction of light as represented by the arrow, render the following forms. Assume the objects are resting on a horizontal surface. Use the pole example to estimate shadow lengths. Render sun, shade, and shadow.

Name:	**Rendering Sketch Sheet**
Class:	Mastering 3D Studio
Date:	

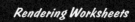

Create geometry as assigned by your instructor. Establish a light source direction and ground shadow. Assign materials and textures as appropriate. Render the scene.

Name:
Class:
Date:

Rendering Sketch Sheet
Mastering 3D Studio

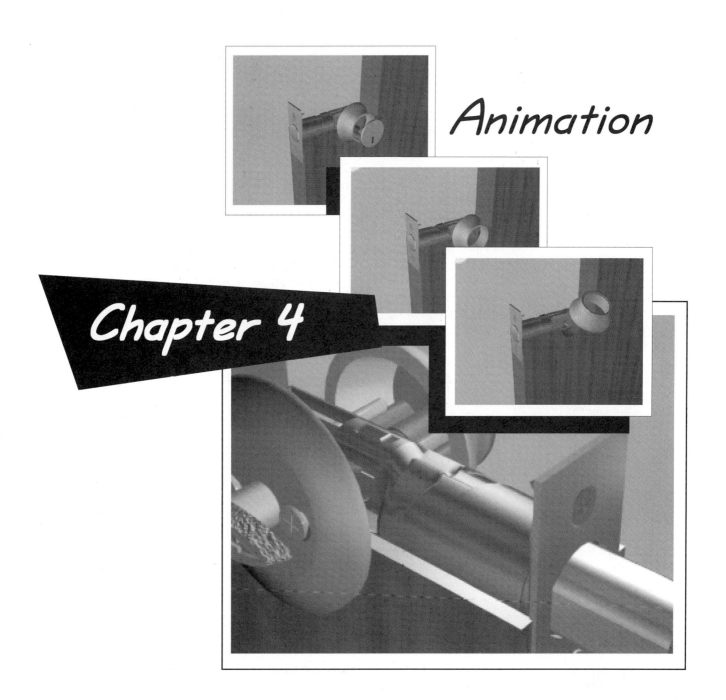

Chapter 4

Animation

4 Animation

4.1 Introduction

Make it move! Make it move! Your primary objective in animation is, after all, to animate! According to Webster, the term animate means "to give natural life to; to make alive." You certainly want to start with valid 3D models and effective materials and lighting. But without a carefully planned and executed motion sequence, all you will have is a nice group of still rendered shots. Animation requires careful study of how objects move, change shape, rotate, and otherwise interact with each other over *time*.

Terms to Know and Define

active animation
field of view (FOV)
filler frames
FLC format
focal length
key frame
morphing
parallax
passive animation

4.2 An Animation as a Stage Play

One of the easiest ways to understand and approach 3D animation is to think of it as creating a story and designing a stage set for a theatrical play. Actors (objects) can move across the stage while the camera traverses, pans, rolls, or pitches; lights can turn on and off, change point of focus, or change color. Figure 4-1 shows a series of frames where actors, lights, and the camera have been transformed. Following is a listing of events that must take place with any successful 3D Studio animation project.

TUTORIAL
1-18 through 1-22

REFERENCE
8-1, Colorplate 44

- ■ *First, you must have a script and a plan.* These will take the form of storyboards and a script describing your vision for the new "play."

- ■ *Once the script and storyboards are created, it's time to build props and stage sets in the form of computer graphic models.* In 3D Studio, computer models are built using the 2D Shaper, 3D Lofter, and 3D Editor program modules. Additionally models may be imported from other programs, such as AutoCAD. Bear in mind that the actors as well as many of the other props in your stage sets will typically be moving 3D computer models.

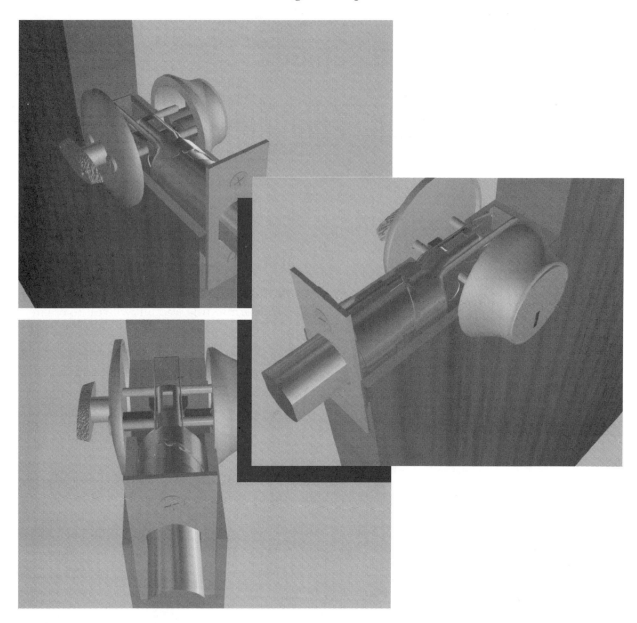

Figure 4-1 **Animation Variables.** When you plan your animation, you have control over time, space, and light.

- **Next, your actors and props will need costumes, makeup, paint, carpeting, and other materials.** In 3D Studio, create these items using the Materials Editor module. Additional customized materials, textures, and bump maps may also be created and imported from a variety of other raster or pixel-based painting programs, from scanners, or from video capture. Final preparation of your specialized materials takes place in the Materials Editor module.

- **Now it's time to paint,** dress (assign customized materials to), and set up your 3D props and "actors" on stage. This process, done in the 3D Editor module, also involves creating and placing lights and setting up cameras.

- **And now, it's time to animate!** This critical event occurs in the Keyframer module and allows you to create a preview or "dress rehearsal" by working out the key frame actions and motions over a time sequence. Time sequences are set by the number of frames between each key frame. The final animation will also be created or "rendered out" in this module.

These last two steps form an animation design loop. That is, in defining camera paths you may decide to alter materials and lights, which may necessitate additional changes in key frames or even in the geometry itself.

4.3 Storyboarding

A storyboard, like that shown in Figure 4-2, is a series of sketches used for planning an animation. Not every frame of the animation requires a sketch. Instead, key frames representing critical points in the animation are planned, allowing the animation program itself to fill in the missing sequences by transforming objects in the scene from one key frame and the next.

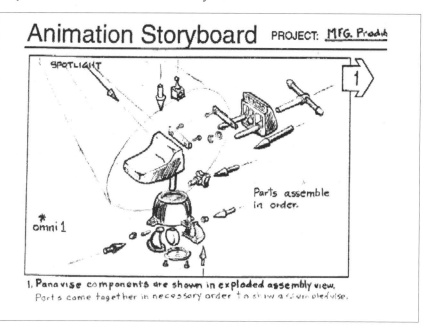

Figure 4-2 **Key Frame Storyboard.** Notice that spatial movement of geometry in the scene, camera position, and lighting considerations enter into the planning.

Every practicing animator knows the role of the storyboard in the process. Your ability to imagine and plan an animation through storyboards is critical in demonstrating your understanding of the process. In professional computer animation, storyboarding offers the following advantages:

>1. ***Storyboards establish a visual reference at the start of a project.*** Effective storyboards enable everyone involved in the project, especially the client and other animators on the team, to visualize what an animation will look like before investing the time and effort in the animation itself. All serious animation requires storyboards.

>2. ***Storyboards serve as a focal point for planning.*** Questions concerning camera position, focal length, object

motion, lighting, materials, and other proposed actions in a scene can be explored quickly in sketch form. Critical decisions can be made with quick action sketches before committing time and expense to the system.

3. Storyboards have little emotional investment. It's a lot easier to throw away a sketch than it is to throw away a 3D Studio model and project file. Animators have a tendency to stay with an animation once it's in the computer, continually tweaking and fiddling with the models, materials, lights, and key frames in hopes of improving the animation. At the beginning of an animation project, you will be more likely to explore creative alternatives in a sketch than in the software.

4.4 Key Frame Animation

The term **key frame** is a carry-over from the way in which early studios, like Walt Disney, created animations. Basically, the senior or master animator(s) would start by designing and laying out the *key* storyboards for an animation; the key storyboards contained pivotal points in the story. Other junior animators

Readings

Tutorial   Tutorial 14

Reference Chapter 8

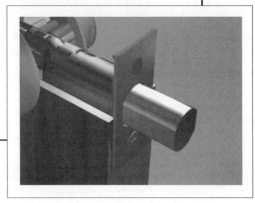

would then create all of the frames that occured in between the key frames.

First, you create key frames, in the Keyframer module, in which important actions occur. A sample action might be a rotating fan blade or the curving path of a ball. Next, the Keyframer automatically calculates all of the frames that occur between each key frame; typically for playback at 30 frames per second.

Learning to do key frame animation requires the ability to work in four dimensions; width, height, depth, plus the fourth dimension of *time*. Figure 4-3 shows the key frames and the automatically calculated **filler frames** for a moving object.

 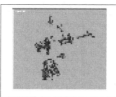  
   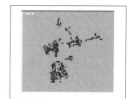
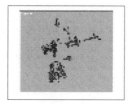   

Figure 4-3 **Key Frames and Calculated Filler Frames.** Each of the key frames was planned by executing a key frame sketch like that shown in Figure 4-2.

4.5 You Must Know the Camera

TUTORIAL

1-22,
14-17 through 14-20

REFERENCE

7-172 through 7-180

The visual relationship between the person watching an animation and the action occurring within the animation may be used to divide animations into two categories: *passive* and *active*.

In a **passive animation** you, the viewer, remain perfectly still while the action occurs all around you. Objects and lights move in and out of the scene while you stand still and watch. You don't move through the scene or even rotate your head; you simply remain in a fixed spot and observe. Passive animations are usually short, specialized, and may be useful for showing physical relationships between movable 3D objects.

In an **active animation**, not only do the objects move but you, the observer, actively move around and through the scene. A simple example of this would be an architectural walk-through. The vehicle that allows the viewer to move through the scene is the camera. Cameras, which may be thought of as the viewer's eyes, are also 3D Studio's primary method of generating and controlling the perspective appearance in a scene.

A camera's perspective parameters can be easily manually adjusted with the Camera/Adjust command. The dialogue box, shown in Figure 4-4, shows the options available for manually adjusting field of view (FOV) and roll, and for selecting camera lenses.

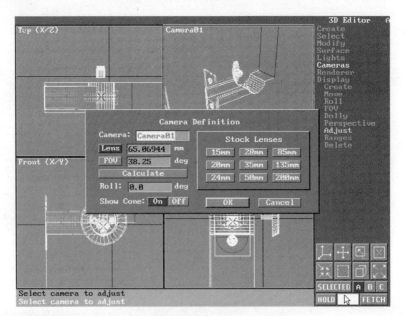

Figure 4-4 **Camera Controls.** By understanding how these controls effect your animation views you can achieve realistic results.

You should follow some general guidelines in the selection of camera variables. Normal perspective is approximated by 55mm of **focal length** when using a 35mm camera. A focal length shorter than 28mm produces dramatically converging perspective. This is called *wide-angle*. Taken to its extreme, very short focal lengths produce curvilinear perspective called *fish eye*. Focal lengths longer than 80mm are called *telephoto* and result in the absence of converging perspective. Taken to the extreme, very long focal lengths result in compressed depth. See Figure 4-5.

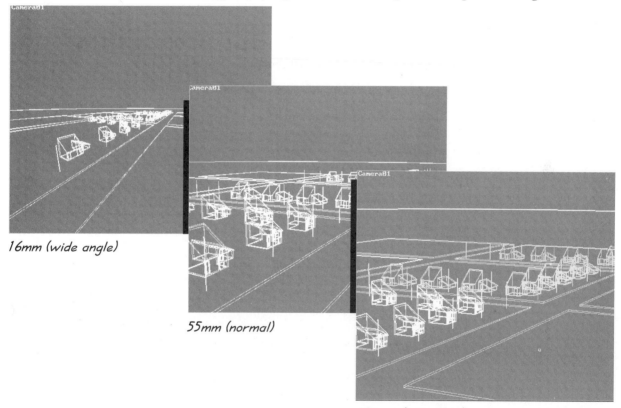

16mm (wide angle)

55mm (normal)

120mm (telephoto)

Figure 4-5 **Effect of Lens Length on View.** *Using the 35mm film format, a 55mm focal length produces a view close to that seen by normal vision. A 16mm lens allows you to be closer to the subject. A 120mm lens brings distant objects closer.*

Most dramatic animations, especially large-scale architectural subjects, use short focal lengths. Very small objects are more effectively animated using a normal (55mm) focal length. As a general rule:

> *Short focal lengths make small objects look larger while long focal lengths make large objects look smaller.*

Field of view (FOV) works with focal length controls and impacts the distortion introduced into an animation. This distortion is often called **parallax**. When distorted, elements become bent or angled as they are removed from the center of focus. FOV is related to focal length in that short lenses (less than 28mm) are associated with wider fields of view. Long lenses are associated with a narrower FOV. Figure 4-6 shows different ways of viewing a scene by adjusting the FOV while keeping the focal length constant. Observe the distortion when FOV is outside the expected range.

4.6 Everything Moves

One of the greatest and most interesting challenges in designing a 3D computer animation is the flexibility to move anything within a scene. In 3D Studio, all objects, lights, cameras, even individual faces may be moved; everything moves! The movements in an animation may be dull and predictable or exciting and interesting. In 3D Studio, the responsibility is yours!

To assist you, key frame planning sheets have been provided in this book. Figure 4-7 relates the key frames to the planning sheet and animation frames.

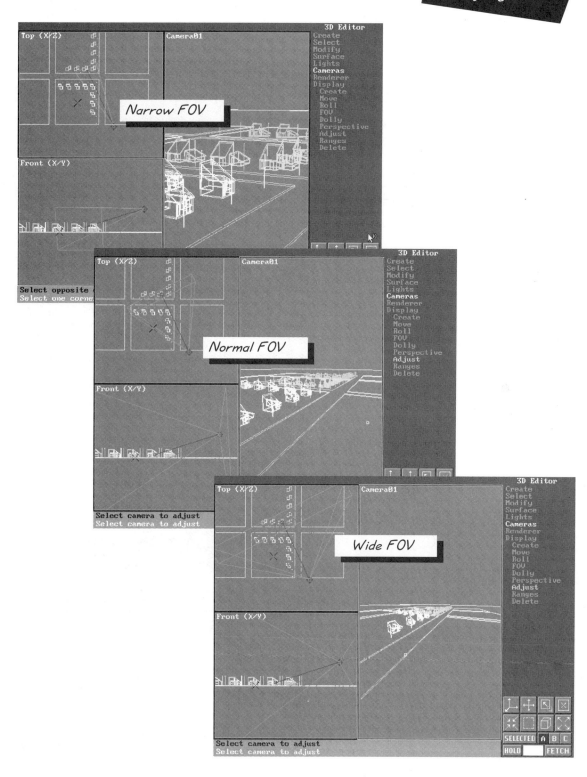

Figure 4-6 ***Change in Field of View.*** *Notice the parallax caused when the included angle of view exceeds the expected values.*

4 Animation

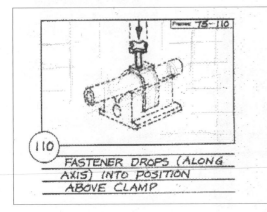

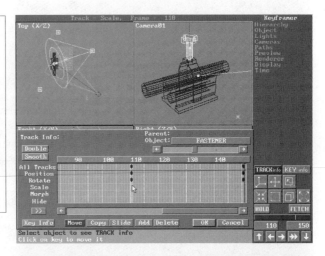

20-8, 20-15 through 20-16

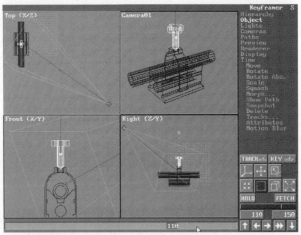

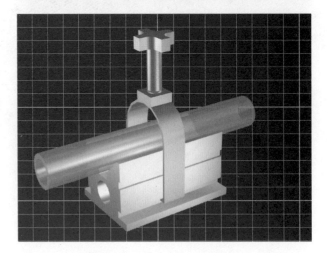

Figure 4-7 **Key Frame Sketches, Key Frames, and Filler Frames.** This figure brings sketching, key framing, and animation together.

4.7 Morphing

16-10 through 16-22

8-59 through 8-63

One of the most popular special effects or visual tricks used in movies and television is the technique of changing one shape into another. In science fiction terms this is called *shape shifting*. The notion of shape shifting has become so popular that the television series *Deep Space Nine* has a character that frequently changes from human form into a picture frame, a chair, or his natural liquid state. In computer graphics and in 3D Studio this technique is called **morphing**. The expression is derived from the term *metamorphosis*, which means to change physical form or shape.

Morphing has been used so extensively for dramatic special effects that most new animators fail to see how it might be used to achieve less spectacular but equally important technical effects. A few examples of how morphing can be used (in addition to changing a butterfly into a lion) include:

- Making a piece of paper appear to curl or roll up into a tube.

- Animating mechanical motions such as a telescoping mechanical arm, a slinky spring, or other complex interrelated mechanical motions.

- Capturing subtle natural movement such as branch or leaf motion on a wind-blown tree or flower.

- Creating minor facial motion such as a twitching nose or a curling lip.

In addition to morphing physical models, another useful technique is 3D Studio's ability to morph materials. This is particularly useful for showing such effects as changing architectural colors, aging a material, or changing the fabric on a piece of furniture. The effect of a simple material morph can be just as dramatic as a total shape shift.

There is a cardinal rule in 3D Studio concerning objects that can be morphed. *All shapes and objects must have the same number of vertices.*

When you use this fundamental rule there are two techniques for creating morphable objects in 3D Studio.

1. Start with the same 2D Shaper outline. Use different paths in the 3D lofter to create different objects. Because the shapes are based on the same 2D profile, each contains the same number of vertices.

2. Clone 3D objects in the 3D Editor. Then manipulate one or both of the objects by scaling or moving individual vertices. Because the shapes are based on the same 3D object, each contains the same number of vertices.

Once a variety—usually three or more morphable objects—has been created, the morphing operation is performed in the Keyframer module by arranging and sequentially assigning each transitional object as a morph target at key frames in the animation. When the animation is rendered, the program will automatically calculate all intervening frames showing the gradual change in the shape and materials of the object. Figure 4-8 shows the result of a series of morphed objects.

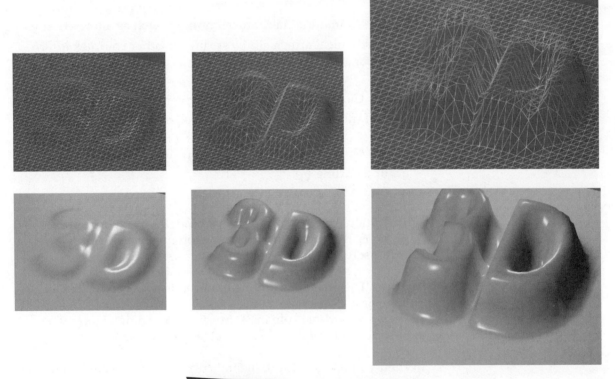

Figure 4-8 **Morphed Objects.** Note that the beginning and ending shapes are based on the same geometry so that morphing can take place.

4.8 Animation Formats

TUTORIAL
14-21

REFERENCE
2-12, 8-115, 7-217

Know These Formats

.fli
.flc
.bmp
.tga
.tif
.jpg
.gif

What is an animation format? Basically, this term refers to the structure of the information used to describe all of the parameters of an animation sequence. The animation file itself is a series of still, raster (bit-mapped) images called *frames* that can be rapidly displayed in succession, usually at the rate of 30 frames per second. The result of viewing the rapid display of sequential frames is animation.

3D Studio offers a variety of formats for creating and storing animations. The two primary animation formats used by 3D Studio are referred to as "flic" files and can be identified by either **.flc** or **.fli** file extensions. A flic file represents a series of **.gif** (256-color raster images) frames that are stored in compressed format. These file formats are similar in that both use an 8-bit, 256-color palette. The **.fli** format is limited to 320 x 200 pixels while **.flc** files can be rendered at any resolution.

In addition to using **.flc** formats for creating animations, you can use any of the supported bit-map types in creating your individual animation frames. Depending on your release of 3D Studio, you may have access to targa (**.tga**), tagged image file format (**.tif**), windows bit map (**.bmp**), and joint photographers exchange group (**.jpg**) raster formats. Graphic interchange format (**.gif**) files are limited to 256 colors while the other files may support up to 16.7 million colors. Preliminary animations should be rendered at the coarsest resolution using the fewest colors necessary to make valid judgements about the animation.

The **.flc** format is used in a large number of other DOS and Windows applications. Recently, Microsoft adopted the **.flc** format as a standard for Windows-based multimedia presentations. You are likely to see many other programs that support your **.flc** animation files.

There are some considerations that you must keep in mind when working with 8-bit, 256-color raster images. With a pallete of only 256 colors you must plan materials, colors, and lighting very carefully in order to get as much out of the color selection as possible. One way to do this is to use colors and materials within the same family of colors. In HLS parlance, the H value shouldn't vary much. Use pastel blue-greens, warm earth tones, or subtle grays. Working with selective color palletes may ultimately make you a better animator.

4.9 Animation Exercises

At the end of this chapter are several animation sketching assignments. They are intended to promote a deeper understanding of key frames and the way they function. These exercises also encourage you to develop your sketching ability. Starting with the next chapter, your model-planning and key-framing sketches must be as professional as you can make them.

4.10 Questions to Answer

1. How can the relationship between focal length and field of view impact visual distortion or parallax?

2. Consider a highly irregular, curved camera path. How does the shape of the path influence the number and placement of key frames or the frame rate?

3. What is the difference between active and passive animation? Propose an example of each.

4. Why does 3D Studio require that both beginning and ending morph shapes have the same number of vertices?

5. Describe the variables that influence the decision of format for frames rendered in an animation.

6. What is file compression? Why is it important? Research several of the most common compression methods and be prepared to discuss strengths and weaknesses of each.

7. Discuss the factors that have a negative impact on animation playback speed.

Animation Sketch Sheet

Plan a one-second, thirty-frame animation from the toolbox to the left. Use 3 x 5 cards to create a flip book from key frames at 0, 15, and 30. Use assignment guidelines provided by your instructor.

Shapes

- BEND
- SUDDEN STOP
- SQUASH
- SPLAT
- TWIST
- DIMPLE
- BEND
- BEND
- SQUASH
- SQUASH
- DEFORM
- SHIMMY
- SHIMMY

Frames: 0

Frames: 15

Frames: 30

Name:
Class:
Date:

Animation Sketch Sheet
Mastering 3D Studio

85

Animation Worksheets

Plan a one-second, thirty-frame animation from the toolbox to the left. Use 3 x 5 cards to create a flip book from key frames at 0, 15, and 30. Use assignment guidelines provided by your instructor.

Shapes

- BEND
- SUDDEN STOP
- SQUASH
- SPLAT
- TWIST
- DIMPLE
- BEND
- BEND
- SQUASH
- SQUASH
- DEFORM
- SHIMMY
- SHIMMY

Frames: 0

Frames: 15

Frames: 30

Name:
Class:
Date:

Animation Sketch Sheet
Mastering 3D Studio

Animation Worksheets

Plan a one-second, thirty-frame animation from the toolbox to the left. Use 3 x 5 cards to create a flip book from key frames at 0, 15, and 30. Use assignment guidelines provided by your instructor.

Shapes

- BEND
- SUDDEN STOP
- SQUASH
- SPLAT
- TWIST
- DIMPLE
- BEND
- BEND
- SQUASH
- SQUASH
- DEFORM
- SHIMMY
- SHIMMY

Frames:

(0)

Frames:

(15)

Frames:

(30)

Name:
Class:
Date:

Animation Sketch Sheet
Mastering 3D Studio

89

Chapter 5

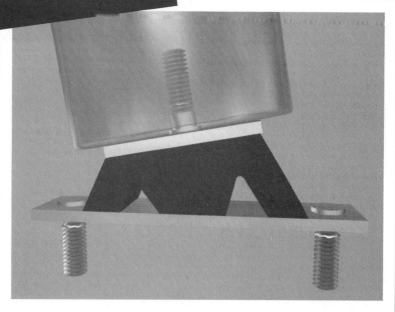

Product Detail

5 Product Detail

5.1 Introduction

We are currently at a crossroad in how companies communicate marketing information about their products. Traditionally, two pieces of technical literature have been used to promote products to technically literate non-engineering customers:

> 1. **The Specification Sheet (Spec Sheet).** A single sheet that identifies features, sizes, and options for a single product or product line. It is used to make a potential customer aware of a product's potential.
>
> 2. **The Manufacturer's Catalog.** A multi-page publication that combines specification sheets and performance data so that the customer can make comparisons between different models or products.

Technical animations are currently being used to supplement these two marketing devices. With an animation, a potential customer can better visualize the form, function, and applicability of a product.

5.2 Your Assignment

Your assignment is to translate the technical information for a *Shock Mount* into a short animation. Working from the manufacturer's catalog pages reproduced in Figure 5-1, create a short (5 to 7 seconds @ 30 frames per second) 3D animation of an M-Style Mounting. Figure 5-2 shows a completed mount in its initial position. The animation is to be used for dynamic customer product visualization and will include the following requirements:

metric — M-Style Mountings

■ FOR STANDARD LOADS OF 33 TO 275 POUNDS

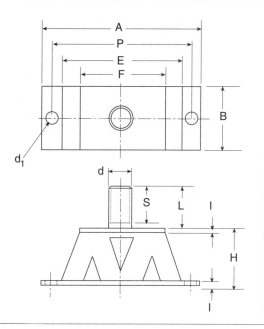

FEATURES
- Compared with circular rubber mountings they ensure lower spring rate in vertical direction and higher stability in horizontal direction.
- Suited for machines which generate considerable vibrations during low speed operation.
- Excellent in controlling vibrations of 600 cpm or higher.
- Can be installed in a very small area because of its narrow width.
- Used for oscillating motions.

APPLICATIONS
- Vibration screen
- Vibration conveyors
- Vibration servos
- Instrument panels
- Refrigerators
- Compressors

MATERIAL: Mounting Plates--Mild Steel Painted
Insulators--Natural Rubber

10 VIBRATION & SHOCK - METRIC -

DIMENSIONS

Catalog Number	A (In)	A (mm)	B (In)	B (mm)	H (In)	H (mm)	I (In)	I (mm)	E (In)	E (mm)	F (In)	F (mm)	P (In)	P (mm)	d	L (In)	L (mm)	S (In)	S (mm)	d1 (In)	d1 (mm)
A10Z45MKD040	4.92	125	1.18	30	1.58	40	0.18	4.5	3.15	80	2.17	55	4.09	104	M10	1.14	29	0.98	25	0.43	11
A10Z46MKD045	6.30	160	1.38	35	1.77	45	0.18	4.5	3.94	100	2.76	70	5.12	130	M12	1.34	34	1.26	55	0.55	14
A10Z46MKD055	8.27	210	1.58	40	2.17	55	0.24	6	5.12	130	3.54	90	6.7	170	M16	2.13	54	1.97	67	0.67	17
A10Z46MKD065	9.65	245	1.97	50	2.56	65	0.32	8	6.51	165	4.53	115	0.07	205	M16	2.05	57	1.97	79	0.79	20

10-53

Figure 5-1 *Shock Mount Specifications.* Use the information in this table to model an M-style mounting.

5 Product Detail

Figure 5-2 **Shock Mount in Initial Position.** Note that the rubber mount has not been deformed. It is done as the mount rotates.

Specifications:

The specifications are equivalent to a client's specifications and contract. Read them carefully.

- Rotate the mount 360 degrees to highlight and display the various geometric features of the part.

- The part geometry itself is to be rotated, not the camera.

- A compression and torsion load is to be applied to the mount, which will cause the rubber mount to deform appropriately.

■ Finished animations should contain between 150 and 210 frames.

5.3 Your Project Notebook

What is a project notebook? This question addresses the same problem that, as an animator, you face in any class: *What should I write down?* At first, write down everything, no matter how silly it seems. There are a few things you should write down or sketch no matter what the assignment.

■ First, write an abstract describing verbally your concept of the animation.

■ Sketch the components of the mount on a *Model Planning Sheet*. This process makes you more familiar with its components so that you can make good modeling decisions later.

■ Next, your storyboards should be sketched and described on your *Animation Storyboard Sheet*.

■ Develop and document a logical file-naming and location system on your *File Organization Sheet*. For each model, write down the file name and where it is located.

■ For each material, write down a description of the material including name and RGB and HLS settings on your *Objects and Materials Sheet*.

■ Develop a simple animation plan. This plan is typically a single sketch showing proposed paths and actions for the animation. Translate this to your *Frame Planning Sheet*.

■ Plan your camera and lights and their targets by working between your storyboards and the *Cameras and Lighting Sheet*.

5.4 Storyboards

Accurate, professionally sketched thumbnails that storyboard the motion for the animation are required. Use a *Storyboard Sheet* from the supply at the end of this book. Include a scripted caption or narrative complete with directional arrows explaining the proposed transformation (squash or rotate). Figure 5-3 shows an appropriate frame from a Shock Mount storyboard.

5.5 Model Construction

The parts for this project can be made in 3D Studio or created in AutoCAD as solid models. In either case, sketch each part using a *Model Planning Sheet*. Use this sketch to plan your modeling strategy. If you use AutoCAD, export the parts as meshed DXF files with a precision of four (4). If you choose to model directly in 3D Studio (and for the purposes of this first exercise that would be fine), determine which shapes can be comprised of primitives, lofted, booleaned, or created directly in the 3D Editor. Figure 5-4 shows a frame in which the rubber mount has been deformed.

Readings

Tutorial   Tutorials 15, 16, & 17

Reference   Chapter 9, pages 9-10 through 9-20

Model Construction

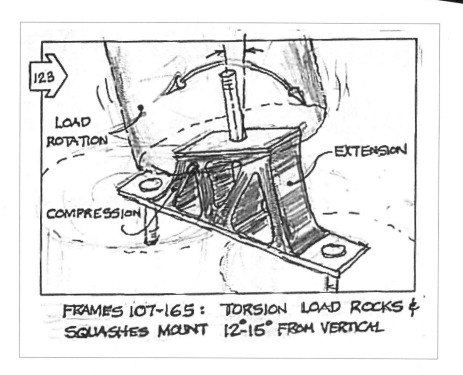

Figure 5-3 Shock Mount Storyboard.

Figure 5-4 Shock Mount Under Compression.

5.6 Scene Layout

Materials:	Your choice from the default materials library
Ambient Light:	Low setting
Omni Lights:	One blue/cyan—left and behind the product
	One magenta/red—right and behind the product
Spotlight:	White—in front and above the product Umbra to completely cover product—20°-30° cone angle
Background:	Neutral solid gray or earth tone

5.7 Animation Setup and Key Frames

Produce an animation clip of the Shock Mount which depicts the visual detail of each part through a series of smooth rotations and pauses.

5.8 Finished Animation Materials

Document your work by saving all appropriate materials in a 3-ring binder. Include your planning sheets from this workbook. Archive the following files to diskette and include in a holder in your 3-ring binder:

- **.prj** the Shock Mount project file
- **.fli** the animation flic file
- **.gif** your best single rendered frame

5.9 Alternative Assignments

1. Choose an object that has an abundance of three-dimensional reliefs, such as grooves, ridges, threads, treads, embossing, engraving, and the like. Perform all operations using bump maps.

2. Choose an object that has cuts or parts removed, such as windows, access panels, portals, etc. Create these openings by using opacity maps exclusively.

3. Choose a product that has a variety of materials, such as chrome, brushed aluminum, matte black plastic, crinkle finish, porcelain, fabric, and wood. Create material and texture maps for each and output on test geometry.

4. Choose an object with compound curved surfaces. Attempt to model the subject using extruded, swept, and meshed objects from the Shaper and Lofter; alternatively, use combinations of scaled primitives in the 3D Editor; finally, use only boolean operations on primitive geometry. Consider the following subjects:

- Aircraft
- Sailboat
- Automobile
- Submarine
- Spacecraft
- Fiberglass Swimming Pool
- Jet Ski

Chapter 6

Product Assembly

6 Product Assembly

6.1 Introduction

Many manufactured products become the subjects of multimedia products for marketing, training, and maintenance. Once modeled, the product can be viewed from any vantage and specialized graphics extracted as needed. Many manufacturers are providing interactive product literature, giving potential customers a much better idea of the form and function of their products.

Animation clips can be integrated into full multimedia presentations. Still frames can be chosen to reveal specific product features and included in traditional print publications.

Study the still frames drawn from product animations in Figure 6-1. From these examples, you should be able choose, model, render, and effectively animate your own product.

6.2 Project Description

You are to select a manufactured product to model and animate. For practicality, you will want to choose a product that can be held in one hand. You may work individually or in teams as assigned by your instructor. To give you the opportunity to produce an effective product animation, consider the following:

1. **Multiple Materials.** Choose a product that has multiple materials such as chrome, brushed metal, painted gloss or semigloss surfaces, or wood grain.

2. **Realistic Geometry.** Choose a product that is within your ability to model. Remember, your job is to create a *rendition* of the product, not a manufacturing data base.

3. **Appropriate Position.** Position the product spatially in a position in which it will normally be used or observed.

Project Description

4. Appropriate Detail Scale. Analyze the product and determine which detail will be discernible at the desired viewing distance. You will need to plan your animation paths *before* modeling so that detail too fine to be seen at the display resolution (640 x 480) is omitted.

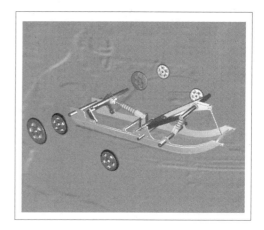
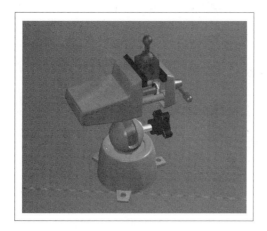
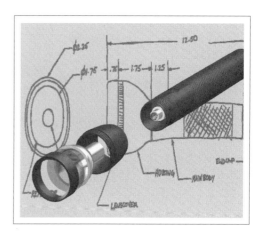

Figure 6-1 **Product Gallery.** These products represent the type and complexity appropriate for this project.

103

6.3 Storyboards

You are to produce accurate, professionally sketched thumbnails storyboarding the motion for the animation. Include a scripted caption or narrative complete with directional arrows explaining the proposed transformations (squash and rotate) for each panel (key frame). A professional rule of thumb: Ten panels are sufficient for a 30-second animation. Use the *Animation Storyboard Sheets* provided.

6.4 Project Notebook

Keep a notebook, including a brief abstract describing your project objective, thumbnail sketches, a job description indicating the name and duties of each team member (if appropriate), an explanation of your file-naming system, and storyboards with script. Storyboard sketches must be completed on storyboard sheets included in this sketchbook and must be turned in with the animation. Sketches must include directional arrows and descriptive text information and must be your best professional effort.

6.5 Model Construction

Models for this project must be constructed in 3D Studio. Parts may be constructed in AutoCAD or another modeling program provided you document the reason 3D Studio was not used. Save each model as a separate .3ds file to facilitate merging it with the project file for assembly and animation. Figure 6-2 shows examples of geometry for several products.

This project may be your first experience in directly measuring a product and translating those measurements into a digital model. Accuracy for this assignment should be ± 1 mm. To improve your efficiency consider the following steps:

> **1. Look for primitive shapes.** Determine the fundamental geometry of the product. Can you use 3D Studio's geometric primitives in combination to create the basic shape? Can boolean operations be applied to these shapes to create more complex forms?

2. Look for extruded (lofted) shapes. Geometries on the product that have consistent cross-sectional shape are candidates for Shaper-Lofter extrusion.

3. Look for swept shapes. Geometries on the product that have symmetrical cross-sectional shapes are candidates for Shaper-Lofter sweeping.

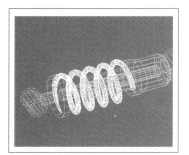 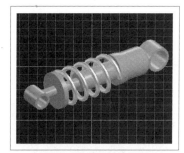 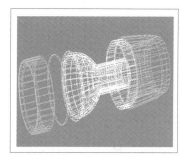
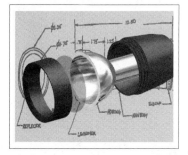 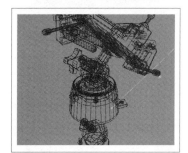 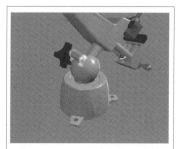

Figure 6-2 **Product Geometry.** Note the use of extruded, swept, and boolean shapes.

6.6 Scene Layout

It is recommended that you create a specific library of materials for this project. Avoid backgrounds that interfere with the primary goal of your animation. Background panels such as floors and walls are discouraged as they may cast shadows that obscure geometric detail. Figure 6-3 shows a scene with cameras and lights. Note the use of light sources and ground and rear planes.

All of these features should be saved as you create your master .prj project file.

Materials:	Your choice from the default materials library. You may modify a material but you must document the modifications.
Camera:	A single camera with focal length of 35mm
Ambient Light:	Low setting
Omni Lights:	As many as are required
Spotlight:	As many as are required
Background:	Neutral solid color. If you opt for a custom background such as a grid or pattern, you must justify your decision.

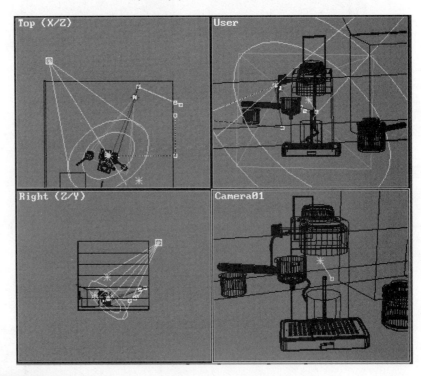

Figure 6-3 ***Product Scene with Cameras and Lights.*** *Note the use of back lighting and cameras placed for up-close detail.*

6.7 Animation Setup and Key Frames

What you do in the Keyframer module must be as consistent as possible with your animation plan. As you make changes in the keyframer, update your notebook and animation plan accordingly. If major changes are required, discuss them with your team members (if you are working in a team) and with your client—in this case, your instructor.

6.8 File Organization

Use the root directory on your hard drive C:\ to temporarily store your files. All files for this project must be named P2-1.eee (eee being the appropriate file extension; for example, .dwg, .dxf, .3ds, .prj, .fli—these extensions are assigned automatically by the program).

Readings

Tutorial   Tutorials 18&19

Reference   Chapter 9

6.9 Finished Materials

Consider that you will be presenting your animation to a client, who expects a professional project report. Anything you do to set your solution apart from others that may be considered increases the possibilities of success. The following materials must be professionally packaged and turned in on completion of the project:

Notebook A black 3-ring binder with a standard information tag centered on the cover and a plastic diskette holder.

Diskettes The completed project must include your .prj file and at least three, but not more than six, still images in .tga format at 640 x 480 resolution. If a file will not fit on a single diskette, use a compression program such as PK-Zip to compress or split up your final work. Label all diskettes clearly and professionally to match the project.

6.10 Alternative Assignments

1. Model an assembly of at least eight (8) parts. Create separate animations intended to be used for the following:

   - Assembly
   - Disassembly
   - Part Identification
   - Disposal

2. Take an assembly you have completed and change the point of view (usually a removed viewer) to be that of one of the parts. Change the direction of the camera as the part is being assembled so that the effect of subsequent parts can be seen.

3. Simulate the failure of a part in an assembly. First assemble the parts. Then operate the assembly, increasing some variable (speed, distance, torque, temperature, etc.) until a part fails. Show the effect of the failure.

4. Model a shipping carton out of folded cardboard for a product you have completed. Show how the product and its supporting literature are packed into the carton.

Chapter 7

Process Model

7 Process Model

7.1 Introduction

In the previous exercise, you modeled and animated the operation of a manufactured product that you could hold in your hands. In this exercise, you will be modeling something much larger—a simplified engineering process model. This project would be similar to a gas, chemical, or petroleum installation.

Depending on how much time you have to devote to this project, and whether or not you are working as part of a group, you may want to model only a portion of the installation. Figure 7-1 shows several details of an electronic process model. Plan and elevation views are included at the end of this chapter. You are encouraged to research standard industrial construction details, fittings, and equipment.

Scale three-dimensional models, made from plastic, wood, and foam, have been commonly used both to design and to document a process installation. Because it is often difficult to determine position and clearances on traditional engineering drawings, these models are often kept in trailers on the construction site where engineers and installers can check component position and make changes as necessary. When construction is complete, the model is often the only exact record of the "as is" condition of the construction. In 3D Studio, an electronic model accomplishes the same function as does this traditional scale model.

TUTORIAL
20-8 through 20-15

REFERENCE
8-84 through 8-90

This assignment is comprised of two phases. *Phase I* requires that you model the process installation. *Phase II* requires that you create an animation that presents the electronic model much as you would view a scale model by walking around it, observing each of the site's major components.

Reproduced for you in this chapter are scaled elevation and plan views of the process installation as well as details of control valves. These are necessarily abstracted from the actual engineering drawings; the massive amount of information not needed to construct the model has been removed. Use the height information for the center lines of tanks, pipes, and frame stations. Scale tank diameters directly.

Introduction

Figure 7-1 **Process Model Details.** These rendered frames show the level of detail appropriate for inclusion in an engineering process model.

7.2 Project Description

Phase I   Modeling Geometric Components

The object of this exercise is to model and animate a simplified engineering process model. The subject for this animation is the refractory section of a refinery.

Your instructor may want to divide your class into groups or teams. If you are working individually on this project, approach the problem by moving from group to group yourself.

- ■ **Group 1: Site Preparation.** Create a level site the size of the construction boundary. Locate the projection of basic center line geometry at ground elevation to help in locating components (Figure 7-2). These guidelines can be deleted before rendering.

- ■ **Group 2: Structural Steel Frames.** Assume that the frame structure is constructed from standard steel angle, tee, I, H, and box members (Figure 7-3). The frame uses a rectangular concrete casing at each vertical member as its foundation.

- ■ **Group 3: Towers, Tanks, and Bases.** You may choose to loft tank and tower shapes or to construct them from primitives in the 3D Editor (Figure 7-4). Create them in principle position, that is, in the position in which they will be installed.

- ■ **Group 4: Piping, Elbows, and Valves.** Model piping by lofting the pipe cross section along the appropriate pipe center line path (Figure 7-5). Allow 3D Studio to determine intersection transitions at rendering time, reducing the need to create boolean intersections. Model only those control valves that will be seen during camera motion.

- ■ **Group 5: Catwalks, Handrails, and Ladders.** Use the information found on the elevation and plan views to locate these features (Figure 7-6). You may want to create a library of standard elements (tread, stringer, pipe rails, etc.).

Project Description

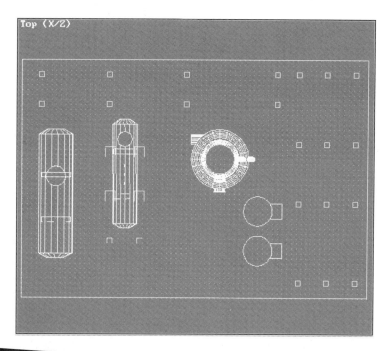

Figure 7-2 **Site Preparation.** Locate the position of major components on a site that conforms to the shape and size of the plot plan.

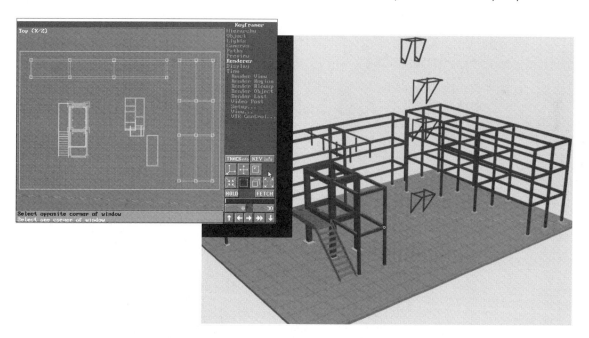

Figure 7-3 **Structural Steel Components.** Analyze the structural steel used in the process plant and create library shapes for lofting.

7 Process Model

Figure 7-4 **Towers and Tanks.** *These components can be modeled using combinations of primitives and structural steel shapes.*

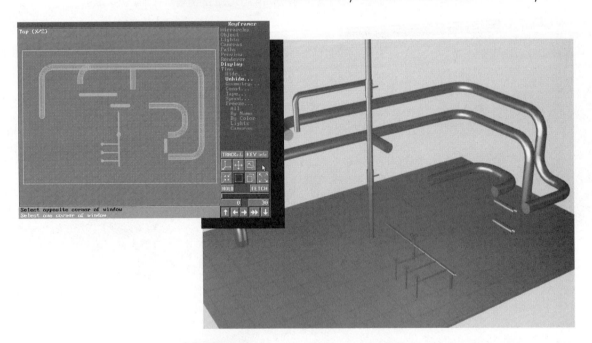

Figure 7-5 **Piping, Elbows, and Valves.** *Loft pipe cross-sectional shape along a path defined by the pipe's center line.*

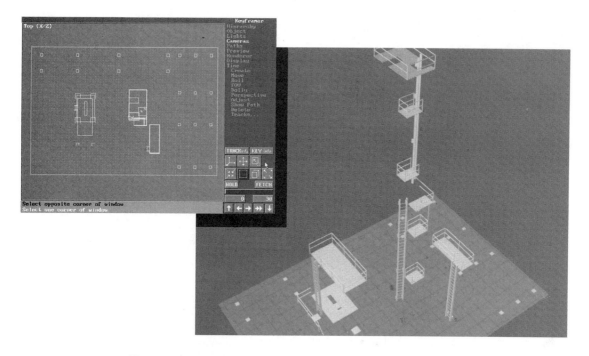

Figure 7-6 *Catwalks, Handrails, and Ladders. Create only those details that will be seen in your animation.*

Phase II   Fly-by Animation

The intended use of this animation is for inclusion in multimedia and/or video for familiarizing staff with the facility's major components. You will want to make one full revolution around the facility before settling the observer on the ground. In your animated walk-through, pace the viewer at a comfortable walking pace (2 mph or approximately 3 feet/sec).

Fly-by: 4 seconds of 360 rotation @ 15 frames per second

Walk-through: 10 seconds of 3 feet per second @ 15 frames per second

7.3 Model Planning Sketch

On the planning sheet provided, sketch a pictorial of the installation looking northeast. Begin by establishing center lines and elevations. Work from general volumes and shapes, refining the forms and finishing line work beginning with Tank A and progressing to the K Frame and pipe.

7.4 Project Notebook

A notebook is required, including a brief abstract describing your project objective, a model planning sketch, a job description indicating the names and duties of each team member (if appropriate), an explanation of your file-naming system, and storyboards with script.

Include all planning sheets as appropriate. Storyboard sketches must be completed on the storyboard sheets included in this sketchbook and must be turned in with the animation. Because this animation moves the camera while the geometry is stationary, the planning of the camera path is very important. You may use your model planning sketch to route the camera path. Use a directional vector to show the direction of sight at key frame locations.

7.5 Storyboards

Storyboards function somewhat differently in a walk-through or fly-over because the model geometry remains passive while the camera moves through the scene as the viewer's eyes. This is an opportunity to use multiple cameras, each with a focal length and a field of view appropriate for each scene or set of scenes. For example, close-up frames of control valves should use 28-35mm lens length with a fairly narrow (10°-20°) field of view. To avoid distortion, longer shots of the process model will appear more realistic if the perspective is less drastic. These shots call for a 55-120mm lens and medium field of view (30°-40°).

You are to produce accurate, professionally sketched thumbnails storyboarding the camera motion for the animation. Storyboards allow you to plan more involved processes, like bump maps. Figure 7-7 shows a bump map and the resulting rendered catwalk texture.

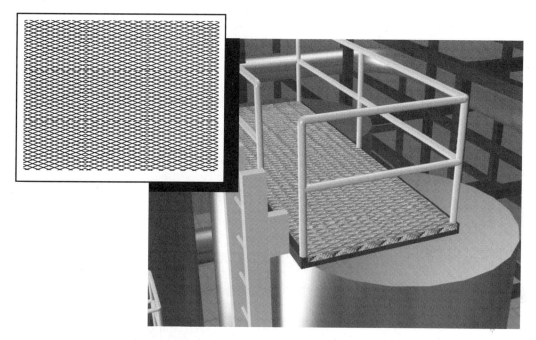

Figure 7-7 **Catwalk Detail.** *The raster bump map shown in the inset panel produces the texture shown in the rendered frame.*

7.6 Scene Layout

This may be your first chance to create a scene with more than one or two materials. You should be careful to choose your materials wisely. Effective materials make use of *contrast*. This contrast can be achieved in two ways. First, you should be after *contrast in value*. If all of your materials have identical light values (HLS model), it will be difficult to determine which objects are in the foreground and which are in the background. Second, you should strive to achieve contrast in hue. If all of your materials are bunched together in the cool (blue) or warm (red) sections of the HLS model, it will be difficult to distinguish one from another.

Materials:
Ground—light gravel
Concrete—contrasts with gravel
Tanks—white painted gloss

	Pipes—stainless steel
	Frames—green metal
	Catwalks, Rails, Ladders—gray metal
Camera:	A single camera with focal length of 28mm
Ambient Light:	Low setting
Omni Lights:	As many as are required
Spotlight:	One main spotlight representing the sun. Position the sun appropriate for mid-morning in the middle of summer for your location. Secondary spotlights as necessary to bring in reflected light.
Background:	Medium blue color.

7.7 File Organization

This exercise will require a fair amount of file management. You will want to model components by type in separate files and assemble them on site. You will probably want to use the file containing the site information as the basis for tanks, pipes, and frames, each in their own .3ds file. Use your *File Organization Sheet* to plan how these files will be brought together.

7.8 Finished Materials

The following materials must be professionally packaged and turned in on completion of the project:

Notebook	A black 3-ring binder with a standard information tag centered on the cover and plastic diskette holder. In this notebook should be your Model Planning Sketch with camera path, storyboards, and one print showing the facility from an aerial vantage. This print can be black and white or color as assigned by your instructor.
Diskettes	The completed project must include your .prj file and at least five still images in .tif or .tga format at 640 x 480 resolution. The set of stills

should highlight a tank, the tower, a pipe intersection, a valve, a stair, the catwalk, and a frame detail.

7.9 Alternative Assignments

1. Develop an animated model showing what happens to an oxygen molecule from the time it enters an automobile engine until its waste is exhausted out the tail pipe.

2. Model one of the following processes:

    - Oil Extraction
    - Lumber Harvesting
    - Bread Making
    - Paper Making
    - Steel Making
    - Glass Making
    - Concrete Mixing
    - Coal Mining (deep mines)
    - Candy Making
    - Spacecraft Launch

3. Create a simulation of an electrical, pnuematic, hydraulic, or mechanical system. Include controls and displays. Pay attention to changes in material states (liquid to gas) or changes in material temperature (such as material under pressure).

4. Create the user interface for an electronic game. Animate the action, including screen, buttons, lights, and any other forms of visual feedback.

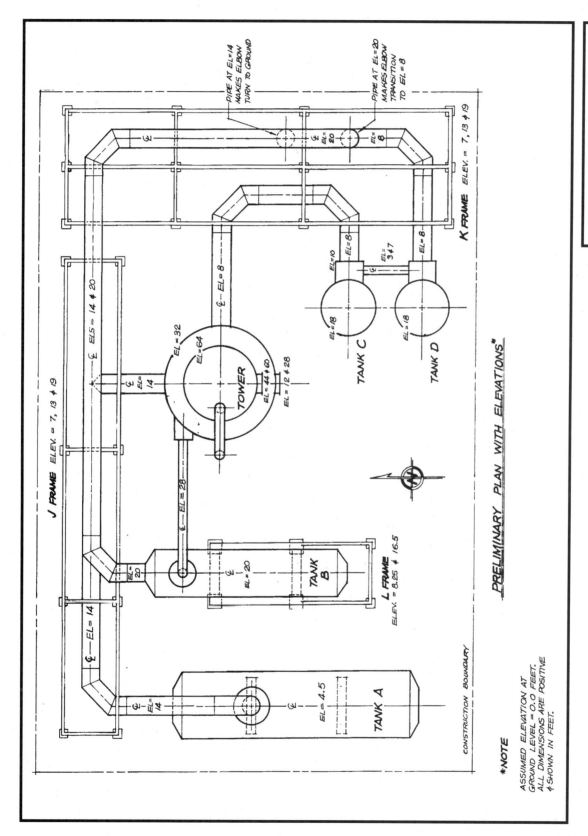

Process Model Plan View
Drawn to Scale

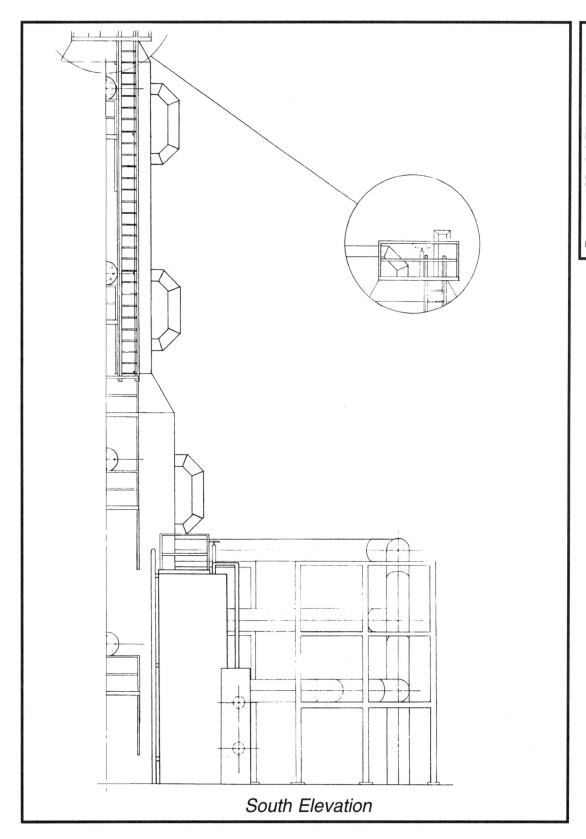

South Elevation

Process Model Elevation Views
Drawn to Scale

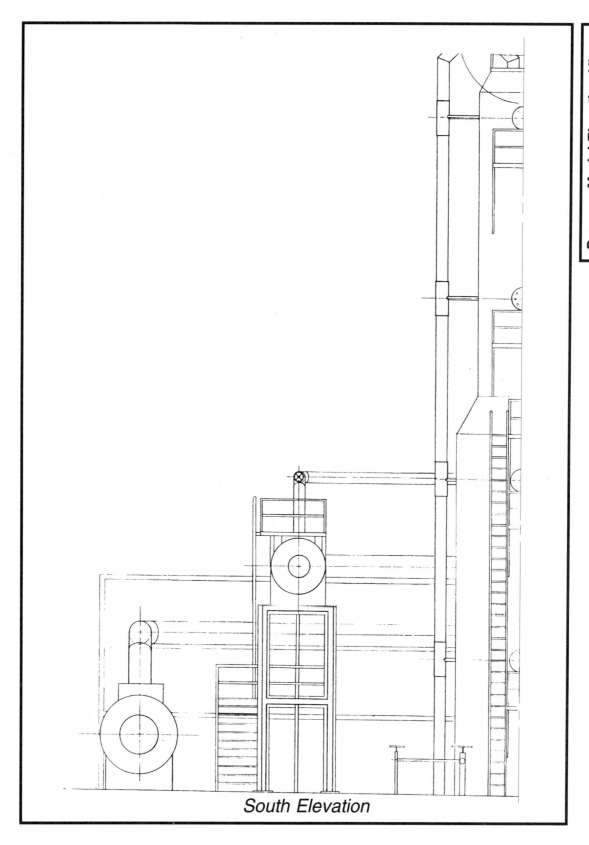

South Elevation

Process Model Elevation Views
Drawn to Scale

Chapter 8

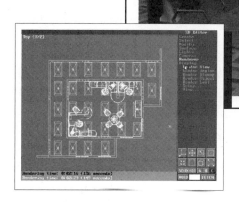

Walk-Through

8 Walk-Through

8.1 Introduction

In the previous chapter, you modeled an engineering process plant. In this exercise, you will model a typical architectural structure and create a path that simulates the view a person would see walking through the space.

This walk-through technique parallels what has been traditionally done by architects and planners for many years—creating scale models out of plastic, wood, and foam core, and either assuming a physical vantage to "eyeball" the space, or photographing the space from desired angles with focal lengths that approximate the cone of vision and depth of field of normal eyesight. Study Figure 8-1, which presents frames from several architectural walk-throughs.

The power of a 3D Studio walk-through lies in several areas:

- *Design Changes.* The design of the space can be altered based on visual information gained during the walk-through.

- *Parameter Changes.* Lighting, materials, and textures can be changed almost in real time to fine-tune the interaction between sun, shadow, materials, and the space geometry.

- *Visual Changes.* The path, direction of sight, and focal length can be altered easily to view the space in the most effective terms.

Reproduced for you in this chapter is a scaled plan view of the space you will be modeling. Use standard architectural detail sizes found in references such as Ramsey and Sleeper's *Architectural Graphic Standards* for wall, door, and window sizes.

Introduction

Figure 8-1 **Architectural Scenes.** Note the effective use of spot and self-illuminating objects that result in realistic renditions.

129

8 Walk-Through

8.2 Project Description

Create a 3D architectural walk-through of the office space shown on the next page and according to the given specifications. Prior to creating the walk-through, your first objective is to design and create a 3D furniture layout for one receptionist and one designer in the office area, utilizing either *Avenir* or *Context furniture systems* from The Steel Case Furniture Company. These products are available in libraries for easy importing into 3D Studio. They are also reproduced in this chapter if you don't have access to the 3D data. The next objective will be to plan and produce a 360- to 480-frame architectural walk-through (preview mode only) of your completed office layout, including at least one loop through the office area. Your final objective will be to produce three (3) rendered .gif still images showing the finished appearance of the area.

8.3 Project Design

1. **Concept Development.** Produce a model planning sketch on the planning paper provided. On this sketch, create your animation camera path and angles, marking key frames at critical positions of change. Produce storyboards detailing at least 5 major positions in the walk-through.

2. **Model Construction.** Construct the floor plan and loft to standard wall height (7'-6"). Creation of a ceiling is optional. If you do create a ceiling, use a single plane for simplicity and to speed rendering. Remember to force 2-sided when rendering the walls.

3. **Rendering Setup.** The assignment of lights and surface materials is up to you with the following architectural restrictions:

    - Floors are to be light- to medium-finished wood, carpeting, or tile (Figure 8-2).

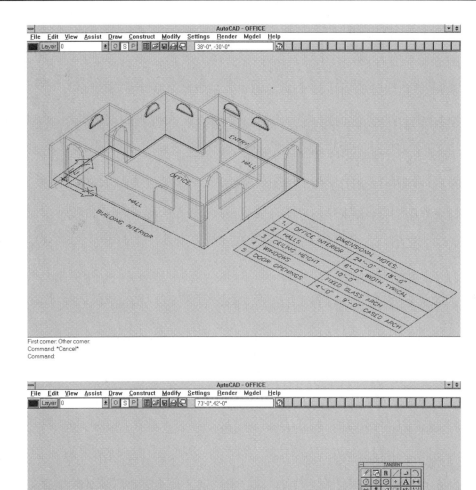
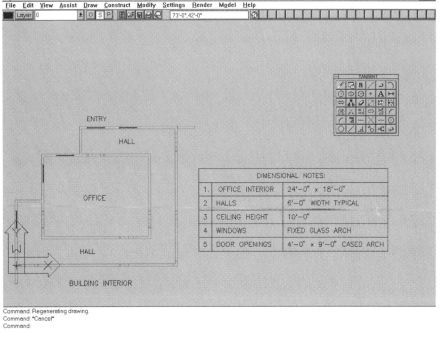

Office Floor Plan and Details
Drawn to Scale

Project Design

Figure 8-2 **Floor and Wall Materials.** *Flooring materials should be light enough to receive shadows yet contrast with walls and furniture.*

- Walls and cased openings for doors and windows are to be a light finish—white or off-white.

- Windows are complementary tinted plate glass with a simple mapped background for sky (Figure 8-3). Arched openings to nowhere are to be planned with the assistance of your instructor.

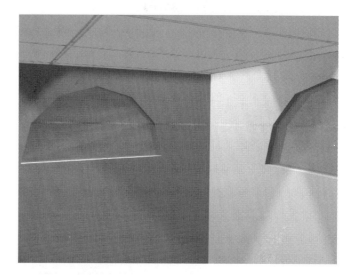

Figure 8-3 **Window Treatment.** *The tinted pane material creates both hue and value contrast with the scene inside the architectural subject.*

8 Walk-Through

- Lighting should consist of a mixture of overhead spot ceiling lights, self-illuminating panels, and color mixtures of lights from various sources to achieve desirable interior lighting conditions. If you use desktop lamps, they must illuminate realistically. Set key lights to cast shadows. Figure 8-4 shows a scene with several light sources.

Figure 8-4 **Lighting Conditions.** *The combination of omni, spot, and self-illuminating surfaces adds sufficient illumination while providing effective contrast.*

Readings

Tutorial Tutorial 20

Reference Colorplates 25, 26

134

4. Animation Setup and Key Frames. The animation camera path should be a continuous loop and must include a clear view of both workcell areas. Adjust camera, camera path, and dolly motion so that the camera view tracks smoothly through the scene. For setup information on cameras for architectural walk-throughs, see Autodesk's 3D Studio *Tutorial Guide*, Tutorial Number 20.

5. Rendered Images and Color Hard Copy. In the package you turn in at the completion of this project include three (3) color still images on disk, 640 x 480 resolution in .gif format. Submit a quality digital color print of the image you feel best shows the model, materials, and lighting, mounted on poster board in quality suitable for exhibition.

Quality Digital Prints
720 dpi Ink Jet
300 dpi Color Laser
300 dpi Thermal Wax
Dye Sublimation

8.4 Model Planning Sketch

On the planning sheet provided at the end of the book, sketch a pictorial of the architectural subject including the following:

- all architectural details including doorways and windows

- workcell furniture in place, using details provided in this chapter

- location of and anticipated falloff from lighting sources

- camera path, direction of sight vectors, and estimated elapsed time between routes and pauses

- notes indicating material choices

8.5 Project Notebook

The following materials will be used to evaluate the success of your architectural walk-through:

- **Model Planning Sketch.** See comments above.

- **File Organization.** Clearly diagram where the model and map components came from.

- **Cameras and Lighting.** Pay close attention to camera and light targets.

- **Objects and Materials.** This may be the first time you personally create a raster texture map in a program such as Photoshop™.

- **Storyboards and Script.** Storyboard sketches and scripts are required and must be turned in with the project. Sketches should include directional arrows and descriptive information and must appear as professional as you are capable of making them.

- **Hi-Res Image Hard Copy.** A color hard copy of a selected frame is required in dye sublimation process. See the side illustration for a suggestion as to how this print should be presented.

- **Frame Planning.** Do you want lights or a computer to turn on as you enter a room or turn off as you exit?

- **Preview Animation.** The preview animation should be turned in, if possible, on a single diskette. Use a program such as PK-Zip, if necessary, to compress the preview.

- **Diskettes.** Professionally labeled diskettes containing the following files must be turned in with the project: a completed project (.prj) file, a .fli or .flc file containing the animation, and three (3) .gif files containing rendered

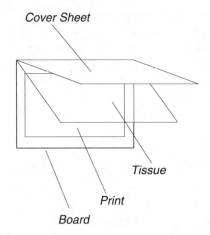

images from the project. Figure 8-5 shows the dimensions and suggested layout for disk labels.

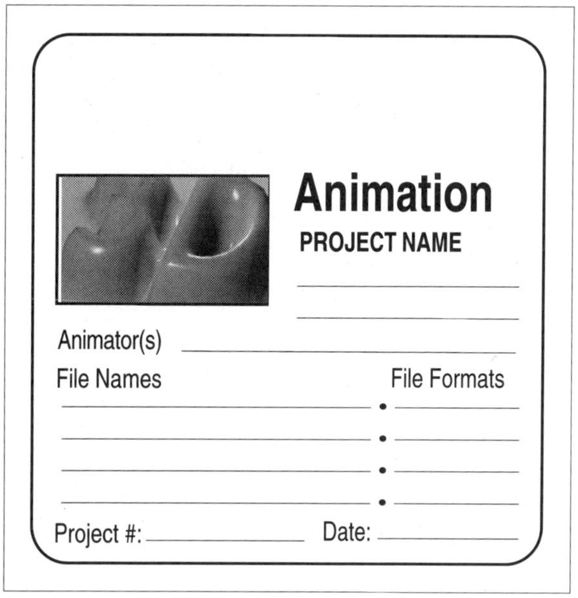

Figure 8-5 *Disk Label. This prototype label for a 3.5" diskette includes all of the information necessary when transporting your animation files.*

8.6 Scene Layout

Materials:	Floor—wood or carpet
	Walls—white or off-white
	Furniture—cloth, wood, matte plastic, and chrome
Camera:	A single camera with focal length of 55mm
Ambient Light:	Medium setting
Omni Lights:	As many as are required
Spotlights:	Appropriate for lighting hallways and workcells
Ceiling Lights:	Self-illuminating panels
Background:	Sky map

8.7 Alternative Assignments

1. Create a walk-through of one of the following:

   - Power Plant
   - Submarine
   - Passenger Aircraft
   - Hospital
   - Residential Structure
   - Storm Sewer

   Place the camera at eye level and assume a normal walking speed.

2. Take the same model and create a fly-over. Create an aircraft window and interior through which you view the scene. Consider the difference between the lighting in an aircraft interior and that outside the aircraft. Is it a sunny day? Cloudy? Stormy?

3. Design and model a roller coaster and a camera path that follows the track. Place the camera in the back car of a four-car train. Put screaming kids in all the seats. Complete one full trip of the track, changing the direction of the camera as appropriate. Include an effective background environment.

Chapter 9

Product Logo

9 Product Logo

9.1 Introduction

Photorealistic animations like those that you have done in 3D Studio are very powerful devices to attract attention. You can probably cite many instances in modern culture where animations have been used to introduce a product or service, grab your attention, inform, or even entertain.

Because this technique can be such an assault on your visual senses, it is often used in a short burst—3 to 5 seconds. Following the animation clip (now that they have your attention!) is the meat of the topic, the news program, sporting event, product pitch, or important information. The animation clip has also been kept short due to economic realities. Until very recently broadcast-quality animations have been *very* expensive. From your experience in 3D Studio, you now know what it takes, in terms of hardware, software, and development time, to produce an animation clip of this length.

In this exercise you will create and animate a logo or commercial name to attract attention and inform. Figure 9-1 shows a gallery of stills from product identification animations.

To avoid any hint of infringement, the use of trademarks, logos, or other registered product identifications in this workbook is for *educational purposes only*. Students who include such materials in their portfolios or videotapes are encouraged to make such a disclaimer.

9.2 Project Description

Select a familiar, nationally known, commercial corporation or organization and secure a reference copy of their logo. Present your selection to your instructor for approval. Using 3D Studio and other software products as necessary, develop a rendered animation that dynamically creates a relationship between the logo, name, and product or service associated with the company. The animation must effectively incorporate the use of 3D objects

Project Description

and motion to achieve a single concept. Finished animations will contain between 90 and 150 frames and last no longer than 5 seconds. This assignment is intentionally open-ended and requires a significant effort in planning and revision *before* modeling and animation commence. The following rules apply to this assignment:

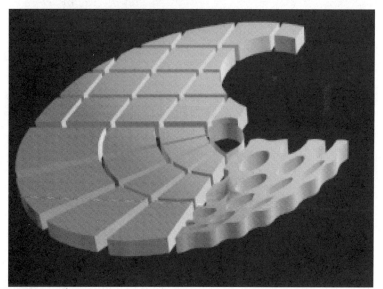

Figure 9-1 **Product Logos.** *The logo may contain the product or an abstraction of the product. Keep all camera and geometry movement appropriate for the product.*

9 Product Logo

> *Rule # 1*   The guidelines in this assignment are equivalent to the client's specifications and contract.
>
> *Rule # 2*   Simplicity almost always means effectiveness.

9.3 *Project Design and Development*

1. ***Concept Development.*** Produce a model planning sketch on the planning paper provided. On this sketch, show how elements of the logo or name are composed or decomposed. Show camera path pictorially as well as the paths of logo elements. When you storyboard the assignment, include 5 key frames with supporting narrative script explaining the proposed transformations for each object in the animation. *Sketches and scripts must be approved by your instructor before you commit time and effort to 3D Studio.*

2. ***Model Construction.*** It is highly recommended that geometry for this animation be constructed within 3D Studio. Other 2D and 3D programs may be used if necessary, as when specialized text outlines are created in a PostScript drawing program (such as Illustrator, Freehand, or Corel Draw!) and imported into 3D Studio's Shaper module.

3. ***Rendering Setup.*** Scene setup and rendering conditions must meet the following specifications:

   - ***Surface Materials.*** Materials are to be chosen from standard 3D Studio materials libraries. Solid and translucent materials are recommended. Texture and bump maps should be used sparingly and only as required.

- **Lighting.** Animations should make maximum use of ambient and omni lighting. Spotlights should be used sparingly and for dramatic effect. Shadows and moving lights should be used only if they are essential for achieving the desired visual effect.

- **Camera.** Use of a single camera is recommended. Lens selection and parallax effects should be appropriately matched with the intended scale of the objects.

4. Animation Setup and Key Frames. Animations may contain any combination of transformations required to achieve the objective of the project. These transformations may include position, rotation, scaling, squashing, and morphing. Timing, tension, continuity, and bias (for velocity and acceleration effects) are critical in producing a smooth and effective animation. Reminder: Concept sketches should show major key frame positions with an explanation of the proposed actions.

5. Rendered Images and Color Hard Copy. In the package you turn in at the completion of this project, include a dye sublimation print of the frame in your animation that completes all transformations. It will probably be the final frame.

9.4 Finished Materials

The following materials will be used to evaluate the success of your architectural walk-through:

- **Planning Sheets.** These must be approved before modeling.

9 Product Logo

- ***Storyboards and Script.*** Storyboard sketches and scripts are required and must be turned in with the project. Sketches should include directional arrows and descriptive information and must appear as professional as you are capable of making them.

- ***Hi-Res Image Hard Copy.*** A color hard copy of the final frame of your animation is required, using dye sublimation process.

- ***Rendered Animation.*** The preview animation should be turned in, if possible, on a single diskette. Use a program such as PK-Zip, if necessary, to compress and split up the preview.

- ***Diskettes.*** Professionally labeled diskettes containing the following files must be turned in with the project: a completed project (.prj) file, a .fli or .flc file containing the animation, and three (3) .gif files containing rendered images from the project.

9.5 Scene Layout

Materials:	Appropriate for your logo choice
Camera:	A single camera with focal length of your choice
Ambient Light:	Medium setting
Omni Lights:	As many as are required
Spotlights:	Appropriate lighting for showing detail
Background:	Your choice from 3D Studio libraries or create your own

9.6 Alternative Assignments

1. Develop a lead-in logo for a television program titled "Ron's Garage." The show is about a part-time mechanic who fixes an old man's '55 Plymouth only to find out later that, when the man dies, the mechanic is named the primary beneficiary of a multimillion dollar estate.

2. Create an animation that morphs a three-dimensional object from its two-dimensional technical drawing. The drawing should be black and white. The object should be its expected color and material.

3. Take a logo you have developed and change its environment. For example, place the logo into a wet environment. Throw the logo into a sandbox. Freeze the logo. Melt the logo. Change a metal logo into glass.

4. Create an animation of a logo that finishes at the beginning key frame so that a seamless loop is created.

5. Create a lead-in animation for TV 43 "Sport's Sillies," a collection of the previous week's most bizarre sports clips.

Index

Symbols

.bmp 83
.flc 83
.fli 83
.gif 83
.prj 105
.tga 83
.tif 83

A

Active animation 76
Add. *See* Boolean operations
Ambient light 46
Analog 2
Animation
    process 2–3
    setup 11
Animator Studio 12
Axis system 26

B

Background 105
Backlighting 52
Bit depth 61
Bitmap 9

Boolean operations 22-23
Box primitive 28
Bulletin board 8
Bump map 24, 54
    alternative to modeling 32

C

CAD 33–34
    model 22
Camera view 26
Clip, in animation 102
Color models 13
Composition 11
Concept development 5–7
Cone primitive 28
Copyright 8
Cylinder primitive 28

D

Digital 2
Diskette 98
DXF format 25, 33

E

Effective rendering 44
Environment 56–57
    map 55
Extrusion 23, 29

F

Field of view   76
Filler frames   75
Filters   44
Fish eye. *See* Focal length
Flat mode   59
Focal length   10, 77
Formats   83
    See also "Symbols" section on p. 146.
Fractel Painter™   53
Fundamental shape   28

G

Global axis system   26
Gouraud mode   60

H

Hemisphere primitive   28
Hierarchical links   11
HLS   13, 95
HOLD   32

I

Intensity of light source   49
Internet   8
Intersection   32

K

Key frame   74–75, 78
    on storyboard sheet   13
Keyframer module   75

L

Lights   49–52
Local axis system   26
Lofted geometry   22
Lofter module   29

M

Maps   7, 55
Materials   6, 9, 52
Materials Editor module   72
Model construction   7
Model geometry   7
Morphing   2, 81–82

N

Native format   48
Notebook contents 7

Index

O

Objects, as actors 70
Omni light 51
Opacity map 24

P

Parallax 78
Parent-child relationships 11
Passive animation 76
Perspective, of camera 76
Phong mode 61
Photorealistic rendering 44, 58–62
Photoshop™ 53
Postprocessing 11
Primitive 23, 28
Profile shape 28
Project notebook 95
Public domain 8

R

Raster 2
Rendering 44–48
    cues 57
    modes 58
    resolution 47
RGB 13, 95

S

Scene layout 9–10
Script 70
Shaper module 26
Sketching 27
Space 26

Sphere primitive 28
Spotlight 46
Still frames 2
Storyboard 6, 70, 72–74, 95
Subtract. *See* Boolean operations
Subtraction 31
Sweeping 23, 30

T

Technical animation 2
Telephoto. *See* Focal length
3D Editor module 26
Tessellation 31
Texture 45
Torus primitive 28
Translation 2

U

Umbra 98
Union. *See* Boolean operations

V

Vector 2
Video capture 54

W

Wide angle. *See* Focal length
Wire mode 59

Gallery

On the next eight pages are examples of work done by Technical Graphics students as they completed the assignments in this book. Their efforts are greatly appreciated. Along with the color figures are references to sections in the 3D Studio *Reference* and *Tutorial Guides*.

Gallery Figure 1. A frame from a walk-through of the engineering process installation assignment found in Chapter 7. Note the use of background bitmap and ground texture. The choice of materials and lighting is critical for depth perception.

| TUTORIAL | 9-16, 13-11 |
| REFERENCE | 7-200, 9-3 |

Gallery

TUTORIAL 15-1, 19-4

REFERENCE 7-52, 7-156

Gallery Figure 2. This frame from a thirty-second product assembly animation from Chapter 6 shows an aircraft with extensible wings. Note the use of transparency maps and a bitmapped background.

TUTORIAL 10-4, 12-6

REFERENCE 7-154, 8-139

Gallery Figure 3. The propellers turn, the background bitmap slowly pans, and the wings retract.

Gallery

Gallery Figure 4. Animating a product detail such as this residential lock can be a challenging solution to the assignment in Chapter 5, both in terms of modeling and component movement.

TUTORIAL 2-34, 15-1

REFERENCE 7-88, 7-173

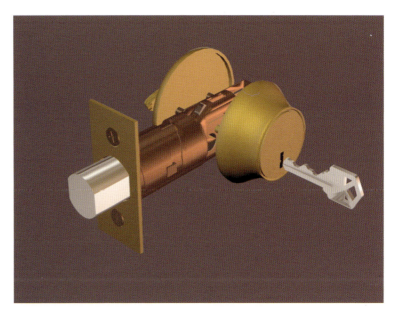

Gallery Figure 5. Completed correctly, the key works the lock, which activates the locking mechanism. An orbiting camera will show how all of the parts interact.

Gallery

Gallery Figure 6. This product animation shows the operation of a vise. Materials are chosen to closely represent the actual materials. The vise is fully functional.

TUTORIAL 20-8

REFERENCE 8-84 through 8-90

Gallery Figure 7. The movement of one component causes the movement of other components because links have been established.

Gallery

Gallery Figure 8. This animation shows the setup and operation of a consumer product. Interior and exterior lights are used to better show material characteristics.

TUTORIAL 12-2, 20-8
REFERENCE 8-139, 9-3

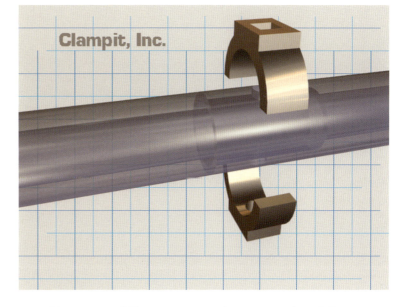

Gallery Figure 9. The product in operation. How many different materials can you identify?

Gallery

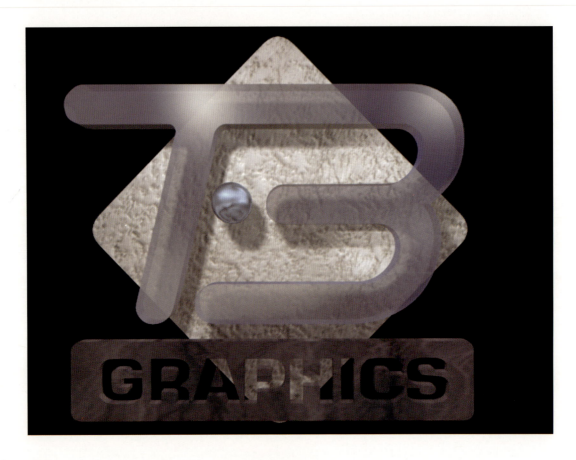

Gallery Figure 10. A corporate logo can combine materials, texture maps, complex geometry, and creative lighting.

TUTORIAL 3-1 through 3-8

REFERENCE 5-2, 6-2, 7-2

Gallery

Gallery Figure 11. The architectural walk-through assignment from Chapter 8 combines materials, textures, lighting, and geometry. A real challenge is to pace the camera so that realistic walking motion is achieved.

TUTORIAL 13-3, 20-11

REFERENCE 7-17, 7-98

Gallery Figure 12. Your walk-through requires that certain components in the scene be illuminated and that you pause to observe them.

Gallery

Gallery Figure 13. A familiar product with its components arranged spatially for assembly. Because many of the components are based on the same module, construction is greatly simplified.

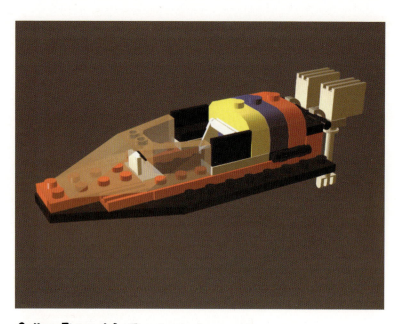

Gallery Figure 14. The finished assembly.

| TUTORIAL | 10-4, 20-8 |
| REFERENCE | 7-98, 9-39 |

Part	Name	Source	Part	Name	Source
○	_____		○	_____	
○	_____		○	_____	
○	_____		○	_____	
○	_____		○	_____	

Description:

Project File Name:

Model Planning Sheet
Mastering 3D Studio

___ of ___

Part	Name	Source		Part	Name	Source
○				○		
○				○		
○				○		
○				○		

Description:

Project File Name:

Model Planning Sheet
Mastering 3D Studio

of

Part	Name	Source	Part	Name	Source
○			○		
○			○		
○			○		
○			○		

Description:

Project File Name:

Model Planning Sheet
Mastering 3D Studio

of

Part	Name	Source	Part	Name	Source
○			○		
○			○		
○			○		
○			○		

Description:

Project File Name:

Model Planning Sheet
Mastering 3D Studio

of

Part	Name	Source	Part	Name	Source
◯	_____		◯	_____	
◯	_____		◯	_____	
◯	_____		◯	_____	
◯	_____		◯	_____	

Description:

Project File Name:

Model Planning Sheet
Mastering 3D Studio

of

Part	Name	Source	Part	Name	Source
○	_____		○	_____	
○	_____		○	_____	
○	_____		○	_____	
○	_____		○	_____	

Description:

Project File Name:

Model Planning Sheet
Mastering 3D Studio

of

Part	Name	Source	Part	Name	Source
◯	_____	_____	◯	_____	_____
◯	_____	_____	◯	_____	_____
◯	_____	_____	◯	_____	_____
◯	_____	_____	◯	_____	_____

Description:

Project File Name:

Model Planning Sheet
Mastering 3D Studio

of

| Frames: | Frames: |

| Frames: | Frames: |

| Frames: | Frames: |

Project File Name:

Animation Storyboard
Mastering 3D Studio

of

| Frames: | Frames: |

Project File Name: | **Animation Storyboard** | of
Mastering 3D Studio

Frames:		Frames:

Frames:		Frames:

Frames:		Frames:

Project File Name:

Animation Storyboard
Mastering 3D Studio

of

Project File Name:	Animation Storyboard
	Mastering 3D Studio

Frames:		Frames:

Project File Name:

Animation Storyboard
Mastering 3D Studio

of

| Frames: | | Frames: |

| Frames: | | Frames: |

| Frames: | | Frames: |

Project File Name:

Animation Storyboard
Mastering 3D Studio

of

Project File Name:

Animation Storyboard
Mastering 3D Studio

of

Project File Name:

Animation Storyboard
Mastering 3D Studio

of

Project File Name:	Animation Storyboard	of
	Mastering 3D Studio	

Frames:		Frames:

Frames:		Frames:

Frames:		Frames:

Project File Name:

Animation Storyboard
Mastering 3D Studio

of

| Frames: | Frames: |

| Frames: | Frames: |

| Frames: | Frames: |

Project File Name:

Animation Storyboard
Mastering 3D Studio

of

Frames:		Frames:

Frames:		Frames:

Frames:		Frames:

Project File Name:	Animation Storyboard	of
	Mastering 3D Studio	

Project File Name:

Animation Storyboard
Mastering 3D Studio

of

Frames:

Frames:

Frames:

Frames:

Frames:

Frames:

Project File Name:

Animation Storyboard
Mastering 3D Studio

of

| Frames: | Frames: |

| Frames: | Frames: |

| Frames: | Frames: |

| Project File Name: | **Animation Storyboard** Mastering 3D Studio | of |

Frames:		Frames:

Project File Name:

Animation Storyboard
Mastering 3D Studio

of

Frames:

Frames:

Frames:

Frames:

Frames:

Frames:

Project File Name:

Animation Storyboard
Mastering 3D Studio

of

Frames:		Frames:

Frames:		Frames:

Frames:		Frames:

Project File Name:	**Animation Storyboard**	of
	Mastering 3D Studio	

| Project File Name: | Animation Storyboard
Mastering 3D Studio | of |

Frames:		Frames:

Frames:		Frames:

Frames:		Frames:

Project File Name:

Animation Storyboard
Mastering 3D Studio

of

Description:	Model Application:
	Raster Application:
	Compression:
	Output Format:

Project File Name:	**File Organization Sheet** Mastering 3D Studio	of

Description:	Model Application:
	Raster Application:
	Compression:
	Output Format:
Project File Name:	**File Organization Sheet** of
	Mastering 3D Studio

Description:	Model Application:
	Raster Application:
	Compression:
	Output Format:
Project File Name:	**File Organization Sheet** Mastering 3D Studio — of

Description:		Model Application:
		Raster Application:
		Compression:
		Output Format:
Project File Name:	**File Organization Sheet**	of
	Mastering 3D Studio	

Description:	Model Application:
	Raster Application:
	Compression:
	Output Format:

Project File Name:	File Organization Sheet	of
	Mastering 3D Studio	

Description: Model Application:

Raster Application:

Compression:

Output Format:

Project File Name:

File Organization Sheet
Mastering 3D Studio

of

Description:		Model Application:
		Raster Application:
		Compression:
		Output Format:
Project File Name:		**File Organization Sheet** of
		Mastering 3D Studio

Light	Position (X-Y-Z)	R	G	B		H	L	S

Camera	Position (X-Y-Z)	Lens (mm)	FOV (deg)

Target	Position (X-Y-Z)

Project File Name:

Cameras and Lighting
Mastering 3D Studio

Light	Position (X-Y-Z)	R	G	B	H	L	S

Camera	Position (X-Y-Z)	Lens (mm)	FOV (deg)

Target	Position (X-Y-Z)

Project File Name:

Cameras and Lighting
Mastering 3D Studio

Light	Position (X-Y-Z)	R	G	B		H	L	S

Camera	Position (X-Y-Z)	Lens (mm)	FOV (deg)

Target	Position (X-Y-Z)

Project File Name:

Cameras and Lighting
Mastering 3D Studio

of

Light	Position (X-Y-Z)	R	G	B	H	L	S

Camera	Position (X-Y-Z)	Lens (mm)	FOV (deg)

Target	Position (X-Y-Z)

Project File Name:

Cameras and Lighting
Mastering 3D Studio

Light	Position (X-Y-Z)	R	G	B		H	L	S

Camera	Position (X-Y-Z)	Lens (mm)	FOV (deg)

Target	Position (X-Y-Z)

Project File Name:

Cameras and Lighting
Mastering 3D Studio

Light	Position (X-Y-Z)	R	G	B	H	L	S

Camera	Position (X-Y-Z)	Lens (mm)	FOV (deg)

Target	Position (X-Y-Z)

Project File Name:

Cameras and Lighting
Mastering 3D Studio

of

Light	Position (X-Y-Z)	R	G	B		H	L	S

Camera	Position (X-Y-Z)	Lens (mm)	FOV (deg)

Target	Position (X-Y-Z)

Project File Name:

Cameras and Lighting
Mastering 3D Studio

Object	Material	R	G	B	H	L	S

Project File Name:

Objects and Materials
Mastering 3D Studio

Object	Material	R	G	B		H	L	S

Project File Name:

Objects and Materials
Mastering 3D Studio

Object	Material	R	G	B		H	L	S

Project File Name:

Objects and Materials
Mastering 3D Studio

Object	Material	R	G	B	H	L	S

Project File Name:

Objects and Materials
Mastering 3D Studio

of

Object	Material	R	G	B	H	L	S

Project File Name:

Objects and Materials
Mastering 3D Studio

Object	Material	R	G	B	H	L	S

Project File Name:

Objects and Materials
Mastering 3D Studio

Object	Material	R	G	B		H	L	S

Project File Name:

Objects and Materials
Mastering 3D Studio

Object/Light/Camera Name			00-09	10-19	20-29	30-39	40-49	50-59	60-69	70-79	80-89	90-99
Material:		Action										
Obj. Type:		Hide										
Material:		Action										
Obj. Type:		Hide										
Material:		Action										
Obj. Type:		Hide										
Material:		Action										
Obj. Type:		Hide										
Material:		Action										
Obj. Type:		Hide										
Material:		Action										
Obj. Type:		Hide										
Material:		Action										
Obj. Type:		Hide										
Material:		Action										
Obj. Type:		Hide										
Material:		Action										
Obj. Type:		Hide										
Material:		Action										
Obj. Type:		Hide										
Material:		Action										
Obj. Type:		Hide										
Material:		Action										
Obj. Type:		Hide										
Material:		Action										
Obj. Type:		Hide										
Material:		Action										
Obj. Type:		Hide										
Material:		Action										
Obj. Type:		Hide										
Material:		Action										
Obj. Type:		Hide										

Action Colors: Translation Rotation Scale Morph

Description:	Material Library:
	Background:
	Palette:
	Page Frame Range:
Project File Name:	**Frame Planning Sheet** — Mastering 3D Studio — of

Object/Light/Camera Name			00-09	10-19	20-29	30-39	40-49	50-59	60-69	70-79	80-89	90-99
Material:		Action										
Obj. Type:		Hide										
Material:		Action										
Obj. Type:		Hide										
Material:		Action										
Obj. Type:		Hide										
Material:		Action										
Obj. Type:		Hide										
Material:		Action										
Obj. Type:		Hide										
Material:		Action										
Obj. Type:		Hide										
Material:		Action										
Obj. Type:		Hide										
Material:		Action										
Obj. Type:		Hide										
Material:		Action										
Obj. Type:		Hide										
Material:		Action										
Obj. Type:		Hide										
Material:		Action										
Obj. Type:		Hide										
Material:		Action										
Obj. Type:		Hide										
Material:		Action										
Obj. Type:		Hide										
Material:		Action										
Obj. Type:		Hide										
Material:		Action										
Obj. Type:		Hide										
Material:		Action										
Obj. Type:		Hide										

Action Colors: Translation _____ Rotation _____ Scale _____ Morph _____ _____

Description:

Material Library:

Background:

Palette:

Page Frame Range:

Project File Name:

Frame Planning Sheet
Mastering 3D Studio

of

Object/Light/Camera Name			00-09	10-19	20-29	30-39	40-49	50-59	60-69	70-79	80-89	90-99
Material:		Action										
Obj. Type:		Hide										
Material:		Action										
Obj. Type:		Hide										
Material:		Action										
Obj. Type:		Hide										
Material:		Action										
Obj. Type:		Hide										
Material:		Action										
Obj. Type:		Hide										
Material:		Action										
Obj. Type:		Hide										
Material:		Action										
Obj. Type:		Hide										
Material:		Action										
Obj. Type:		Hide										
Material:		Action										
Obj. Type:		Hide										
Material:		Action										
Obj. Type:		Hide										
Material:		Action										
Obj. Type:		Hide										
Material:		Action										
Obj. Type:		Hide										
Material:		Action										
Obj. Type:		Hide										
Material:		Action										
Obj. Type:		Hide										
Material:		Action										
Obj. Type:		Hide										
Material:		Action										
Obj. Type:		Hide										

Action Colors: Translation _____ Rotation _____ Scale _____ Morph _____ _____

Description:	Material Library:
	Background:
	Palette:
	Page Frame Range:
Project File Name:	**Frame Planning Sheet** — Mastering 3D Studio — of

Object/Light/Camera Name			00-09	10-19	20-29	30-39	40-49	50-59	60-69	70-79	80-89	90-99
Material:		Action										
Obj. Type:		Hide										
Material:		Action										
Obj. Type:		Hide										
Material:		Action										
Obj. Type:		Hide										
Material:		Action										
Obj. Type:		Hide										
Material:		Action										
Obj. Type:		Hide										
Material:		Action										
Obj. Type:		Hide										
Material:		Action										
Obj. Type:		Hide										
Material:		Action										
Obj. Type:		Hide										
Material:		Action										
Obj. Type:		Hide										
Material:		Action										
Obj. Type:		Hide										
Material:		Action										
Obj. Type:		Hide										
Material:		Action										
Obj. Type:		Hide										
Material:		Action										
Obj. Type:		Hide										
Material:		Action										
Obj. Type:		Hide										
Material:		Action										
Obj. Type:		Hide										
Material:		Action										
Obj. Type:		Hide										

Action Colors: Translation   Rotation   Scale   Morph

Description:

Material Library:
Background:
Palette:
Page Frame Range:

Project File Name:

Frame Planning Sheet
Mastering 3D Studio

of

Object/Light/Camera Name		00-09	10-19	20-29	30-39	40-49	50-59	60-69	70-79	80-89	90-99
Material: Obj. Type:	Action Hide										
Material: Obj. Type:	Action Hide										
Material: Obj. Type:	Action Hide										
Material: Obj. Type:	Action Hide										
Material: Obj. Type:	Action Hide										
Material: Obj. Type:	Action Hide										
Material: Obj. Type:	Action Hide										
Material: Obj. Type:	Action Hide										
Material: Obj. Type:	Action Hide										
Material: Obj. Type:	Action Hide										
Material: Obj. Type:	Action Hide										
Material: Obj. Type:	Action Hide										
Material: Obj. Type:	Action Hide										
Material: Obj. Type:	Action Hide										
Material: Obj. Type:	Action Hide										
Material: Obj. Type:	Action Hide										

Action Colors: Translation   Rotation   Scale   Morph

Description:

Material Library:

Background:

Palette:

Page Frame Range:

Project File Name:

Frame Planning Sheet
Mastering 3D Studio

of

Object/Light/Camera Name			00-09	10-19	20-29	30-39	40-49	50-59	60-69	70-79	80-89	90-99
Material:		Action										
Obj. Type:		Hide										
Material:		Action										
Obj. Type:		Hide										
Material:		Action										
Obj. Type:		Hide										
Material:		Action										
Obj. Type:		Hide										
Material:		Action										
Obj. Type:		Hide										
Material:		Action										
Obj. Type:		Hide										
Material:		Action										
Obj. Type:		Hide										
Material:		Action										
Obj. Type:		Hide										
Material:		Action										
Obj. Type:		Hide										
Material:		Action										
Obj. Type:		Hide										
Material:		Action										
Obj. Type:		Hide										
Material:		Action										
Obj. Type:		Hide										
Material:		Action										
Obj. Type:		Hide										
Material:		Action										
Obj. Type:		Hide										
Material:		Action										
Obj. Type:		Hide										
Material:		Action										
Obj. Type:		Hide										

Action Colors: Translation　　Rotation　　Scale　　Morph

Description:

Material Library:

Background:

Palette:

Page Frame Range:

Project File Name:

Frame Planning Sheet
Mastering 3D Studio

of

Frame Planning Sheet
Mastering 3D Studio

Object/Light/Camera Name

			00-09	10-19	20-29	30-39	40-49	50-59	60-69	70-79	80-89	90-99
Material:		Action										
Obj. Type:		Hide										
Material:		Action										
Obj. Type:		Hide										
Material:		Action										
Obj. Type:		Hide										
Material:		Action										
Obj. Type:		Hide										
Material:		Action										
Obj. Type:		Hide										
Material:		Action										
Obj. Type:		Hide										
Material:		Action										
Obj. Type:		Hide										
Material:		Action										
Obj. Type:		Hide										
Material:		Action										
Obj. Type:		Hide										
Material:		Action										
Obj. Type:		Hide										
Material:		Action										
Obj. Type:		Hide										
Material:		Action										
Obj. Type:		Hide										
Material:		Action										
Obj. Type:		Hide										
Material:		Action										
Obj. Type:		Hide										
Material:		Action										
Obj. Type:		Hide										
Material:		Action										
Obj. Type:		Hide										

Action Colors: Translation _____ Rotation _____ Scale _____ Morph _____ _____ _____

Description:

Material Library:
Background:
Palette:
Page Frame Range:

Project File Name:

____ of ____

Object/Light/Camera Name		00-09	10-19	20-29	30-39	40-49	50-59	60-69	70-79	80-89	90-99
Material:	Action										
Obj. Type:	Hide										
Material:	Action										
Obj. Type:	Hide										
Material:	Action										
Obj. Type:	Hide										
Material:	Action										
Obj. Type:	Hide										
Material:	Action										
Obj. Type:	Hide										
Material:	Action										
Obj. Type:	Hide										
Material:	Action										
Obj. Type:	Hide										
Material:	Action										
Obj. Type:	Hide										
Material:	Action										
Obj. Type:	Hide										
Material:	Action										
Obj. Type:	Hide										
Material:	Action										
Obj. Type:	Hide										
Material:	Action										
Obj. Type:	Hide										
Material:	Action										
Obj. Type:	Hide										
Material:	Action										
Obj. Type:	Hide										
Material:	Action										
Obj. Type:	Hide										
Material:	Action										
Obj. Type:	Hide										

Action Colors: Translation | Rotation | Scale | Morph

Description:

Material Library:
Background:
Palette:
Page Frame Range:

Project File Name:

Frame Planning Sheet
Mastering 3D Studio

of

Object/Light/Camera Name			00-09	10-19	20-29	30-39	40-49	50-59	60-69	70-79	80-89	90-99
Material:		Action										
Obj. Type:		Hide										
Material:		Action										
Obj. Type:		Hide										
Material:		Action										
Obj. Type:		Hide										
Material:		Action										
Obj. Type:		Hide										
Material:		Action										
Obj. Type:		Hide										
Material:		Action										
Obj. Type:		Hide										
Material:		Action										
Obj. Type:		Hide										
Material:		Action										
Obj. Type:		Hide										
Material:		Action										
Obj. Type:		Hide										
Material:		Action										
Obj. Type:		Hide										
Material:		Action										
Obj. Type:		Hide										
Material:		Action										
Obj. Type:		Hide										
Material:		Action										
Obj. Type:		Hide										
Material:		Action										
Obj. Type:		Hide										
Material:		Action										
Obj. Type:		Hide										
Material:		Action										
Obj. Type:		Hide										

Action Colors: Translation _____ Rotation _____ Scale _____ Morph _____ _____

Description:	Material Library:
	Background:
	Palette:
	Page Frame Range:
Project File Name:	**Frame Planning Sheet** — Mastering 3D Studio — of

	Object/Light/Camera Name			00-09	10-19	20-29	30-39	40-49	50-59	60-69	70-79	80-89	90-99
Material:			Action										
Obj. Type:			Hide										
Material:			Action										
Obj. Type:			Hide										
Material:			Action										
Obj. Type:			Hide										
Material:			Action										
Obj. Type:			Hide										
Material:			Action										
Obj. Type:			Hide										
Material:			Action										
Obj. Type:			Hide										
Material:			Action										
Obj. Type:			Hide										
Material:			Action										
Obj. Type:			Hide										
Material:			Action										
Obj. Type:			Hide										
Material:			Action										
Obj. Type:			Hide										
Material:			Action										
Obj. Type:			Hide										
Material:			Action										
Obj. Type:			Hide										
Material:			Action										
Obj. Type:			Hide										
Material:			Action										
Obj. Type:			Hide										
Material:			Action										
Obj. Type:			Hide										
Material:			Action										
Obj. Type:			Hide										

Action Colors: Translation ____ Rotation ____ Scale ____ Morph ____ ____ ____

Description:

Material Library:

Background:

Palette:

Page Frame Range:

Project File Name:

Frame Planning Sheet
Mastering 3D Studio

of

Object/Light/Camera Name			00-09	10-19	20-29	30-39	40-49	50-59	60-69	70-79	80-89	90-99
Material:		Action										
Obj. Type:		Hide										
Material:		Action										
Obj. Type:		Hide										
Material:		Action										
Obj. Type:		Hide										
Material:		Action										
Obj. Type:		Hide										
Material:		Action										
Obj. Type:		Hide										
Material:		Action										
Obj. Type:		Hide										
Material:		Action										
Obj. Type:		Hide										
Material:		Action										
Obj. Type:		Hide										
Material:		Action										
Obj. Type:		Hide										
Material:		Action										
Obj. Type:		Hide										
Material:		Action										
Obj. Type:		Hide										
Material:		Action										
Obj. Type:		Hide										
Material:		Action										
Obj. Type:		Hide										
Material:		Action										
Obj. Type:		Hide										
Material:		Action										
Obj. Type:		Hide										
Material:		Action										
Obj. Type:		Hide										

Action Colors: Translation ___ Rotation ___ Scale ___ Morph ___ ___

Description:

Material Library:
Background:
Palette:
Page Frame Range:

Project File Name:

Frame Planning Sheet
Mastering 3D Studio

of

Object/Light/Camera Name			00-09	10-19	20-29	30-39	40-49	50-59	60-69	70-79	80-89	90-99
Material:		Action										
Obj. Type:		Hide										
Material:		Action										
Obj. Type:		Hide										
Material:		Action										
Obj. Type:		Hide										
Material:		Action										
Obj. Type:		Hide										
Material:		Action										
Obj. Type:		Hide										
Material:		Action										
Obj. Type:		Hide										
Material:		Action										
Obj. Type:		Hide										
Material:		Action										
Obj. Type:		Hide										
Material:		Action										
Obj. Type:		Hide										
Material:		Action										
Obj. Type:		Hide										
Material:		Action										
Obj. Type:		Hide										
Material:		Action										
Obj. Type:		Hide										
Material:		Action										
Obj. Type:		Hide										
Material:		Action										
Obj. Type:		Hide										
Material:		Action										
Obj. Type:		Hide										
Material:		Action										
Obj. Type:		Hide										

Action Colors: Translation   Rotation   Scale   Morph

Description:

Project File Name:

Material Library:
Background:
Palette:
Page Frame Range:

Frame Planning Sheet
Mastering 3D Studio

of

Frame Planning Sheet
Mastering 3D Studio

Object/Light/Camera Name		00-09	10-19	20-29	30-39	40-49	50-59	60-69	70-79	80-89	90-99
Material: Obj. Type:	Action Hide										
Material: Obj. Type:	Action Hide										
Material: Obj. Type:	Action Hide										
Material: Obj. Type:	Action Hide										
Material: Obj. Type:	Action Hide										
Material: Obj. Type:	Action Hide										
Material: Obj. Type:	Action Hide										
Material: Obj. Type:	Action Hide										
Material: Obj. Type:	Action Hide										
Material: Obj. Type:	Action Hide										
Material: Obj. Type:	Action Hide										
Material: Obj. Type:	Action Hide										
Material: Obj. Type:	Action Hide										
Material: Obj. Type:	Action Hide										
Material: Obj. Type:	Action Hide										
Material: Obj. Type:	Action Hide										

Action Colors: Translation | Rotation | Scale | Morph

Description:

Project File Name:

Material Library:
Background:
Palette:
Page Frame Range:

of

Object/Light/Camera Name			00-09	10-19	20-29	30-39	40-49	50-59	60-69	70-79	80-89	90-99
Material:		Action										
Obj. Type:		Hide										
Material:		Action										
Obj. Type:		Hide										
Material:		Action										
Obj. Type:		Hide										
Material:		Action										
Obj. Type:		Hide										
Material:		Action										
Obj. Type:		Hide										
Material:		Action										
Obj. Type:		Hide										
Material:		Action										
Obj. Type:		Hide										
Material:		Action										
Obj. Type:		Hide										
Material:		Action										
Obj. Type:		Hide										
Material:		Action										
Obj. Type:		Hide										
Material:		Action										
Obj. Type:		Hide										
Material:		Action										
Obj. Type:		Hide										
Material:		Action										
Obj. Type:		Hide										
Material:		Action										
Obj. Type:		Hide										
Material:		Action										
Obj. Type:		Hide										
Material:		Action										
Obj. Type:		Hide										

Action Colors: Translation   Rotation   Scale   Morph

Description:	Material Library:
	Background:
	Palette:
	Page Frame Range:
Project File Name:	**Frame Planning Sheet** of
	Mastering 3D Studio

Object/Light/Camera Name		00-09	10-19	20-29	30-39	40-49	50-59	60-69	70-79	80-89	90-99
Material: Obj. Type:	Action Hide										
Material: Obj. Type:	Action Hide										
Material: Obj. Type:	Action Hide										
Material: Obj. Type:	Action Hide										
Material: Obj. Type:	Action Hide										
Material: Obj. Type:	Action Hide										
Material: Obj. Type:	Action Hide										
Material: Obj. Type:	Action Hide										
Material: Obj. Type:	Action Hide										
Material: Obj. Type:	Action Hide										
Material: Obj. Type:	Action Hide										
Material: Obj. Type:	Action Hide										
Material: Obj. Type:	Action Hide										
Material: Obj. Type:	Action Hide										
Material: Obj. Type:	Action Hide										
Material: Obj. Type:	Action Hide										

Action Colors: Translation ___ Rotation ___ Scale ___ Morph ___ ___ ___

Description:

Material Library:
Background:
Palette:
Page Frame Range:

Project File Name:

Frame Planning Sheet
Mastering 3D Studio

of

Object/Light/Camera Name			00-09	10-19	20-29	30-39	40-49	50-59	60-69	70-79	80-89	90-99
Material:		Action										
Obj. Type:		Hide										
Material:		Action										
Obj. Type:		Hide										
Material:		Action										
Obj. Type:		Hide										
Material:		Action										
Obj. Type:		Hide										
Material:		Action										
Obj. Type:		Hide										
Material:		Action										
Obj. Type:		Hide										
Material:		Action										
Obj. Type:		Hide										
Material:		Action										
Obj. Type:		Hide										
Material:		Action										
Obj. Type:		Hide										
Material:		Action										
Obj. Type:		Hide										
Material:		Action										
Obj. Type:		Hide										
Material:		Action										
Obj. Type:		Hide										
Material:		Action										
Obj. Type:		Hide										
Material:		Action										
Obj. Type:		Hide										
Material:		Action										
Obj. Type:		Hide										
Material:		Action										
Obj. Type:		Hide										

Action Colors: Translation   Rotation   Scale   Morph

Description:

Material Library:

Background:

Palette:

Page Frame Range:

Project File Name:

Frame Planning Sheet
Mastering 3D Studio

of

Object/Light/Camera Name			00-09	10-19	20-29	30-39	40-49	50-59	60-69	70-79	80-89	90-99
Material:		Action										
Obj. Type:		Hide										
Material:		Action										
Obj. Type:		Hide										
Material:		Action										
Obj. Type:		Hide										
Material:		Action										
Obj. Type:		Hide										
Material:		Action										
Obj. Type:		Hide										
Material:		Action										
Obj. Type:		Hide										
Material:		Action										
Obj. Type:		Hide										
Material:		Action										
Obj. Type:		Hide										
Material:		Action										
Obj. Type:		Hide										
Material:		Action										
Obj. Type:		Hide										
Material:		Action										
Obj. Type:		Hide										
Material:		Action										
Obj. Type:		Hide										
Material:		Action										
Obj. Type:		Hide										
Material:		Action										
Obj. Type:		Hide										
Material:		Action										
Obj. Type:		Hide										

Action Colors: Translation   Rotation   Scale   Morph

Description:

Material Library:

Background:

Palette:

Page Frame Range:

Project File Name:

Frame Planning Sheet
Mastering 3D Studio

of

Frame Planning Sheet
Mastering 3D Studio

Object/Light/Camera Name

			00-09	10-19	20-29	30-39	40-49	50-59	60-69	70-79	80-89	90-99
Material:		Action										
Obj. Type:		Hide										
Material:		Action										
Obj. Type:		Hide										
Material:		Action										
Obj. Type:		Hide										
Material:		Action										
Obj. Type:		Hide										
Material:		Action										
Obj. Type:		Hide										
Material:		Action										
Obj. Type:		Hide										
Material:		Action										
Obj. Type:		Hide										
Material:		Action										
Obj. Type:		Hide										
Material:		Action										
Obj. Type:		Hide										
Material:		Action										
Obj. Type:		Hide										
Material:		Action										
Obj. Type:		Hide										
Material:		Action										
Obj. Type:		Hide										
Material:		Action										
Obj. Type:		Hide										
Material:		Action										
Obj. Type:		Hide										
Material:		Action										
Obj. Type:		Hide										
Material:		Action										
Obj. Type:		Hide										

Action Colors: Translation ____ Rotation ____ Scale ____ Morph ____ ____

Description:

Material Library:
Background:
Palette:
Page Frame Range:

Project File Name:

___ of ___

Object/Light/Camera Name			00-09	10-19	20-29	30-39	40-49	50-59	60-69	70-79	80-89	90-99
Material:		Action										
Obj. Type:		Hide										
Material:		Action										
Obj. Type:		Hide										
Material:		Action										
Obj. Type:		Hide										
Material:		Action										
Obj. Type:		Hide										
Material:		Action										
Obj. Type:		Hide										
Material:		Action										
Obj. Type:		Hide										
Material:		Action										
Obj. Type:		Hide										
Material:		Action										
Obj. Type:		Hide										
Material:		Action										
Obj. Type:		Hide										
Material:		Action										
Obj. Type:		Hide										
Material:		Action										
Obj. Type:		Hide										
Material:		Action										
Obj. Type:		Hide										
Material:		Action										
Obj. Type:		Hide										
Material:		Action										
Obj. Type:		Hide										
Material:		Action										
Obj. Type:		Hide										
Material:		Action										
Obj. Type:		Hide										

Action Colors: Translation Rotation Scale Morph

Description:

Material Library:

Background:

Palette:

Page Frame Range:

Project File Name:

Frame Planning Sheet
Mastering 3D Studio

of

	Object/Light/Camera Name			00-09	10-19	20-29	30-39	40-49	50-59	60-69	70-79	80-89	90-99
Material: Obj. Type:		Action Hide											
Material: Obj. Type:		Action Hide											
Material: Obj. Type:		Action Hide											
Material: Obj. Type:		Action Hide											
Material: Obj. Type:		Action Hide											
Material: Obj. Type:		Action Hide											
Material: Obj. Type:		Action Hide											
Material: Obj. Type:		Action Hide											
Material: Obj. Type:		Action Hide											
Material: Obj. Type:		Action Hide											
Material: Obj. Type:		Action Hide											
Material: Obj. Type:		Action Hide											
Material: Obj. Type:		Action Hide											
Material: Obj. Type:		Action Hide											
Material: Obj. Type:		Action Hide											
Material: Obj. Type:		Action Hide											

Action Colors: Translation ___ Rotation ___ Scale ___ Morph ___ ___ ___

Description:	Material Library:
	Background:
	Palette:
	Page Frame Range:
Project File Name:	**Frame Planning Sheet** / of
	Mastering 3D Studio

Object/Light/Camera Name		00-09	10-19	20-29	30-39	40-49	50-59	60-69	70-79	80-89	90-99
Material:	Action										
Obj. Type:	Hide										
Material:	Action										
Obj. Type:	Hide										
Material:	Action										
Obj. Type:	Hide										
Material:	Action										
Obj. Type:	Hide										
Material:	Action										
Obj. Type:	Hide										
Material:	Action										
Obj. Type:	Hide										
Material:	Action										
Obj. Type:	Hide										
Material:	Action										
Obj. Type:	Hide										
Material:	Action										
Obj. Type:	Hide										
Material:	Action										
Obj. Type:	Hide										
Material:	Action										
Obj. Type:	Hide										
Material:	Action										
Obj. Type:	Hide										
Material:	Action										
Obj. Type:	Hide										
Material:	Action										
Obj. Type:	Hide										
Material:	Action										
Obj. Type:	Hide										
Material:	Action										
Obj. Type:	Hide										

Action Colors: Translation Rotation Scale Morph

Description:

Material Library:

Background:

Palette:

Page Frame Range:

Project File Name:

Frame Planning Sheet
Mastering 3D Studio

of

	Object/Light/Camera Name		00-09	10-19	20-29	30-39	40-49	50-59	60-69	70-79	80-89	90-99
Material:		Action										
Obj. Type:		Hide										
Material:		Action										
Obj. Type:		Hide										
Material:		Action										
Obj. Type:		Hide										
Material:		Action										
Obj. Type:		Hide										
Material:		Action										
Obj. Type:		Hide										
Material:		Action										
Obj. Type:		Hide										
Material:		Action										
Obj. Type:		Hide										
Material:		Action										
Obj. Type:		Hide										
Material:		Action										
Obj. Type:		Hide										
Material:		Action										
Obj. Type:		Hide										
Material:		Action										
Obj. Type:		Hide										
Material:		Action										
Obj. Type:		Hide										
Material:		Action										
Obj. Type:		Hide										
Material:		Action										
Obj. Type:		Hide										
Material:		Action										
Obj. Type:		Hide										
Material:		Action										
Obj. Type:		Hide										

Action Colors: Translation ____ Rotation ____ Scale ____ Morph ____ ____

Description:	Material Library:
	Background:
	Palette:
	Page Frame Range:

Project File Name:

Frame Planning Sheet
Mastering 3D Studio

of

Object/Light/Camera Name			00-09	10-19	20-29	30-39	40-49	50-59	60-69	70-79	80-89	90-99
Material:		Action										
Obj. Type:		Hide										
Material:		Action										
Obj. Type:		Hide										
Material:		Action										
Obj. Type:		Hide										
Material:		Action										
Obj. Type:		Hide										
Material:		Action										
Obj. Type:		Hide										
Material:		Action										
Obj. Type:		Hide										
Material:		Action										
Obj. Type:		Hide										
Material:		Action										
Obj. Type:		Hide										
Material:		Action										
Obj. Type:		Hide										
Material:		Action										
Obj. Type:		Hide										
Material:		Action										
Obj. Type:		Hide										
Material:		Action										
Obj. Type:		Hide										
Material:		Action										
Obj. Type:		Hide										
Material:		Action										
Obj. Type:		Hide										
Material:		Action										
Obj. Type:		Hide										
Material:		Action										
Obj. Type:		Hide										

Action Colors: Translation ____   Rotation ____   Scale ____   Morph ____   ____

Description:

Material Library:

Background:

Palette:

Page Frame Range:

Project File Name:

Frame Planning Sheet
Mastering 3D Studio

of

Object/Light/Camera Name			00-09	10-19	20-29	30-39	40-49	50-59	60-69	70-79	80-89	90-99
Material:		Action										
Obj. Type:		Hide										
Material:		Action										
Obj. Type:		Hide										
Material:		Action										
Obj. Type:		Hide										
Material:		Action										
Obj. Type:		Hide										
Material:		Action										
Obj. Type:		Hide										
Material:		Action										
Obj. Type:		Hide										
Material:		Action										
Obj. Type:		Hide										
Material:		Action										
Obj. Type:		Hide										
Material:		Action										
Obj. Type:		Hide										
Material:		Action										
Obj. Type:		Hide										
Material:		Action										
Obj. Type:		Hide										
Material:		Action										
Obj. Type:		Hide										
Material:		Action										
Obj. Type:		Hide										
Material:		Action										
Obj. Type:		Hide										
Material:		Action										
Obj. Type:		Hide										
Material:		Action										
Obj. Type:		Hide										

Action Colors: Translation Rotation Scale Morph

Description:

Material Library:

Background:

Palette:

Page Frame Range:

Project File Name:

Frame Planning Sheet
Mastering 3D Studio

of